FOR

WITH

lots of kisses

FROM

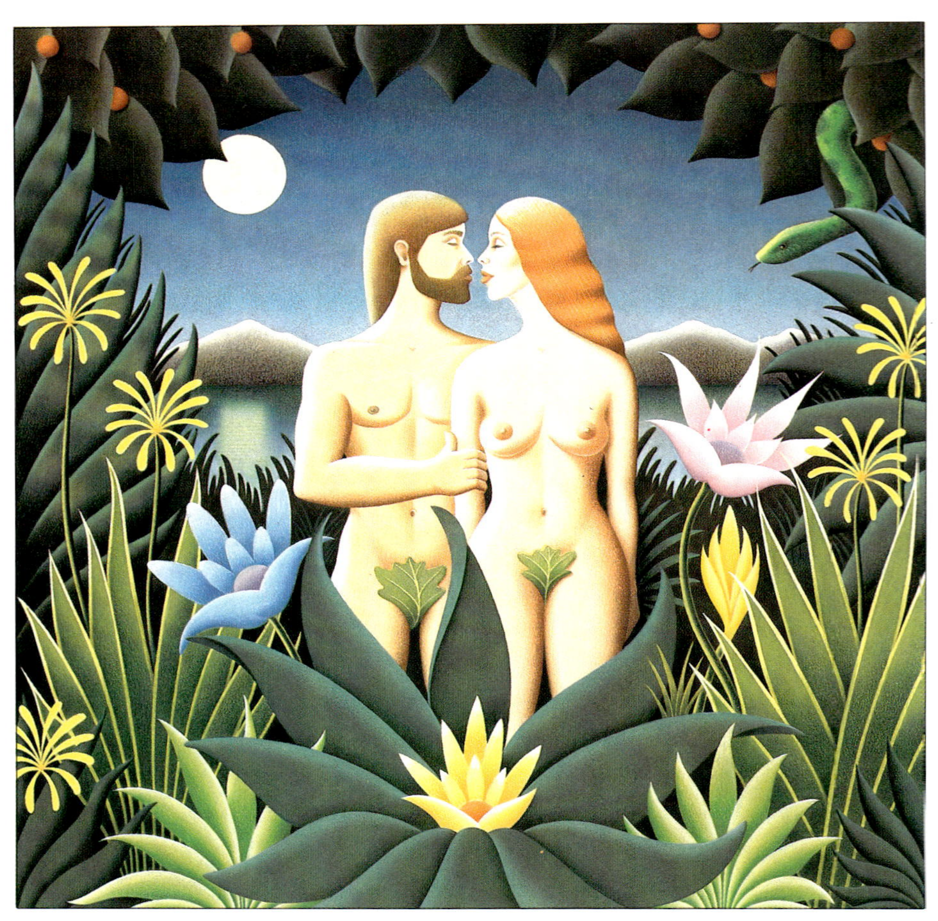

FORBIDDEN KISS

KEITH LABAN

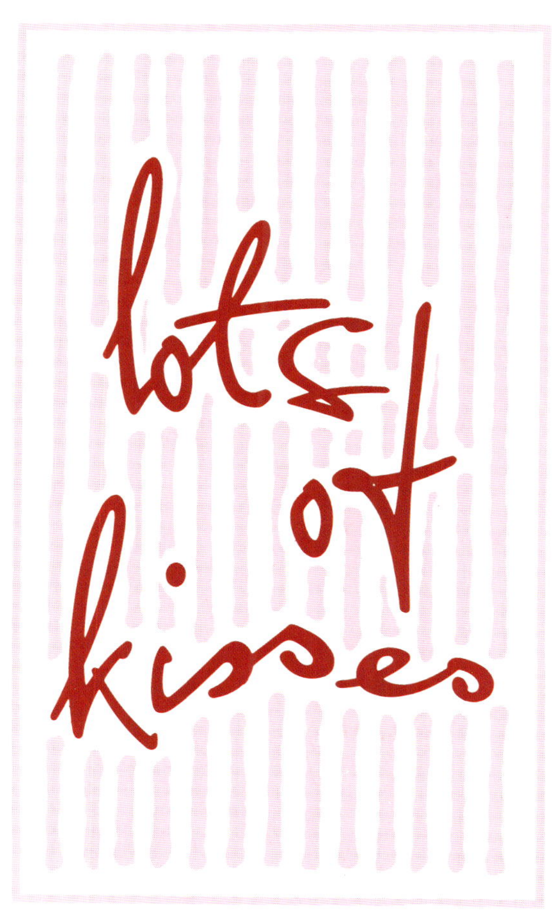

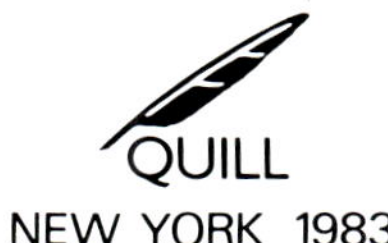
QUILL
NEW YORK 1983

First published in Great Britain by Dragon's World Ltd.

The Publishers wish to thank Chris Meiklejohn, of Meiklejohn Illustration, without whom this book would not have been possible.

Library of Congress Catalog Card Number: 83-62085

ISBN 0-688-02188-3 (pbk)

Printed in Italy

First U.S. Edition

1 2 3 4 5 6 7 8 9 10

Designed by Julie and Steve Ridgeway, assisted by Frank Barron.

Cover illustration by Syd Brak.

COVER GIRL KISS SYD BRAK
FORBIDDEN KISS KEITH LABAN
FIRST KISS PETE KELLY
FAIRYTALE KISS PETER NEAME
KISSES FOR SALE MARTIN GASCOIGNE
KISSING TIME ED STEWART
RELUCTANT KISS DAVID HOLMES
KISS AND MAKE UP KEITH LABAN
COMIC-STRIP KISS JOHN MAC
DRIVE-IN KISS BRIAN JAMES
REFLECTIVE KISS NIGEL TIDMAN
ELECTRIC KISS SYD BRAK
SPORTING KISS PHIL LITTLER
COMPUTER KISS ED STEWART
KOOL KATZ KISS ANDREW FARLEY
KISS AND TELL BRIAN JAMES
KISS ME KWICK GAVIN MACLEOD
EROTIC KISS SYD BRAK
SCREEN KISS JOHN MAC
COPYCAT KISS WARREN MADILL
SEDUCTIVE KISS GARETH WILLIAMS
SEALED WITH A KISS GERRY PRESTON
FOOLISH KISS IRVINE PEACOCK
COWBOY KISS WARREN MADILL
PRIMEVAL KISS JOHN MAC
CRINGING KISS WARREN MADILL
LONG - DISTANCE KISS SYD BRAK
SUN-KISSED DAVID HOLMES
INSTANT KISS PETE KELLY
WET KISS JEFF CUMMINGS
MERMAID KISS ANDREW FARLEY
PRINCELY KISS IRVINE PEACOCK
KISS OF DEATH SYD BRAK
COSMIC KISS PETE KELLY
CLASSIC KISS BARRY LEPARD
HOMECOMING KISS PAUL SIMMONS
FRENCH KISS ROGER PEARCE
FAREWELL KISS PAUL SIMMONS
ONE GREAT KISS FOR MANKIND BARRY LEPARD

ARTISTS FEATURED

SYD BRAK started as an Art Director in Kenya, then moved to South Africa to take up the post of Creative Director for a leading Johannesburg advertising agency. He turned to illustration and moved to London in 1978, joining Meiklejohn Illustration in 1980.

JEFF CUMMINS was born in North Wales in 1954 and studied at Flincher College of Art, North Wales. After college he worked in an advertising agency for two years and then freelanced, mainly in the publishing and music field, joining Meiklejohn Illustration in 1980. When not painting he enjoys music and playing football.

ANDREW FARLEY was born in Epsom, Surrey, in 1956 and educated at Epsom College. After a one-year foundation course at Kingston Polytechnic he took a BA in Graphic Design with illustrative bias, leaving in 1979 to become a freelance illustrator. He joined an artists' agency, working mainly on record covers and paperbacks, then moved to Meiklejohn Illustration in 1982 to work in advertising. His favourite pastimes are watching TV, visiting quaint country pubs, sailing and motorcycling.

MARTIN GASCOIGNE was born in Redhill, Surrey, in 1957. He took a foundation course in art at Kingston College of Art and a degree course in Graphic Art and Design at the London School of Printing, leaving with first class honors to join Meiklejohn Illustration. He is interested in all sports, especially athletics, and plays rugby for his home town of Margate.

DAVID HOLMES was born in Wales in 1954 and studied Graphic Design at the London College of Printing, where he was especially influenced by the work of American illustrators, including Wilson McLean, Mark English and Bob Peak. He turned to freelance illustration in 1980, working at first on magazines and book jackets, and more recently on advertising, using a technique combining airbrush and colored pencil. His wife, Sue, is also an illustrator.

BRIAN JAMES was born in Birmingham in 1947 and trained in Graphic Design at Birmingham College of Art, where he won a national Letraset Student Design competition, and also did graphic work for BBC Television. On leaving college he worked for a Birmingham advertising agency until 1971, when he moved to a Leicester agency where he became Art Director. Growing interest in illustration led him to become freelance, joining Meiklejohn Illustration in 1977. He is married with a son and a daughter.

PETE KELLY was born in 1948 and educated at Southend Art College. He started work in an art studio as an illustrator without having to go through the pain of washing out the more senior artists' water pots, and joined Meiklejohn Illustration in 1975. Known in London as the Airbrush Wizard, he enjoys golf, and is married with a three-year old daughter, four cats and twenty fish.

KEITH LABAN was born in Hackney, London, in 1949, his father a freelance illustrator. He studied at Reigate College of Art, gaining an honors diploma in Illustration and Graphic Design, and was awarded the Sir Alec Issignonis Prize for art. After college he concentrated mainly on magazine illustration and paperback jackets for England and the USA, joining Meiklejohn Illustration in 1977. He lives in Surrey with two cats, two Old English Sheepdogs and a wife.

BARRY LEPARD was born in Pinner, Middlesex, and studied at the Harrow School of Art for four years. He went freelance after working in several art studios, and joined Meiklejohn Illustration in 1982. He adores motor racing and sports cars and is married with three cats.

PHIL LITTLER was born in Ruislip, Middlesex, in 1957, and studied Art at Maidstone College. After working in animation with Dragon for four years he went freelance and joined Meiklejohn Illustration in 1983. When not painting he plays the guitar.

JOHN MAC was born in Glasgow, Scotland, in 1983 and was awarded a four year scholarship to Glasgow School of Art, specializing in commercial illustration. While there he entered two competitions against final year students and won both. On leaving college he worked for a Glasgow advertising agency, then made the great trek South to discover London wasn't paved with gold. After working in a number of art studios he joined Meiklejohn Illustration. He loves golf and the huge American car he occasionally drives when he's not working.

WARREN MADILL was born in 1944, studied at the Hornsey and Slade schools of art and took a Diploma course in Aesthetics at Keele University. He became interested in the technique of old masters and the materials used. Disenchanted with the lack of specific instruction on the subject he started making meticulous copies to see how they did it, then opened a gallery called the "Fine Art Fake Shop" which caused quite a stir in the art world. He now lives in Dorset, working for advertising, publishing and private commissions.

GAVIN MACLEOD was born in Inverness, Scotland, in 1951, but moved to Leeds when he was ten years old. He studied Design and Art at Jacob Kramer, Leeds, and on leaving college worked for two years in an art studio. Now established as Europe's leading car illustrator, he divides his time between being an Art Director of a leading North of England advertising agency, a freelance illustrator for Meiklejohn Illustration, and such leisure pursuits as motor racing, photography and model making.

PETER NEAME was born in Frimley, Surrey, in 1957 and studied at West Surrey College of Art and Design, majoring in Animation and television graphics. Since then he has worked mainly in the animation field as a freelance designer for such companies as Grand Slam, Bob Godfrey Studios and Richard Williams, and joined Meiklejohn Illustration to form an animation department. He is a keen musician, playing guitar and saxophone and collecting blues records.

ROGER PEARCE was born in Kingston in 1943 and educated at Wimbledon Grammar School. Self-taught, he started work in an art studio when he left school, went freelance and joined Meiklejohn Illustration in 1980. His interests include music, jazz guitar and walking.

GERRY PRESTON was born in London in 1935 and studied Art at Twickenham Art College. Upon leaving college he was unable to find a job as an illustrator so he worked as a ladder maker for a year until an art studio vacancy came up, followed by several others, until he went freelance in 1972 and joined Meiklejohn Illustration. He enjoys breeding Japanese carp, photography and travel.

IRVINE PEACOCK was born in Lincoln in 1948, and after a BA in Fine Art Painting from Sheffield College of Art, he took a postgraduate course at Hornsey College of Art. His work has been exhibited extensively in England and Germany and hangs in public and private collections in the United Kingdom, Germany and the USA. He joined Meiklejohn Illustration in 1979.

PAUL SIMMONS was born in 1951. He studied at St Martin's School of Art but left the course for a career in publishing, starting "Wild West Monthly", fully illustrated by himself. After the magazine failed he did illustration work for other magazines, eventually joining John Gilchrist's studio as star illustrator. He turned freelance in 1979, specializing in scenes of dramatic realism, such as film posters. He likes living dangerously, and indulges in martial arts, combat pistol shooting and driving a very fast English sports car. He is married with a baby son.

ED STEWART was born in 1952, and after wasting time in libraries, steel erecting, hod carrying and general building laboring work went to Hornsey College of Art to study Art and Design. He started working freelance while still at college, eventually joining Meiklejohn Illustration in 1982. His hobbies are rock and roll and crashing Porsche motor cars (three to date). He is married with three children.

NIGEL TIDMAN was born in 1942 in Abingdon, Oxford. He started work as an articled clerk but was fired for drawing in the ledgers, then joined a publishing house as a general artist, but fired himself as there was not enough opportunity to draw. He then joined an art studio and learnt how to use an airbrush but left because everybody wanted to retouch photographs and he wanted to draw. He finally went freelance and joined Meiklejohn Illustration in 1976. He also enjoys photography, radio-controlled model aircraft, golf, and taking his car to pieces and putting it back together. He is married with two children and an unpleasant cat.

GARETH WILLIAMS was born in 1956 and educated at Haberdashers Askes School, Elstree. He left the London College of Printing with a BA Honors degree in Graphic Design and joined Meiklejohn Illustration in 1980. Apart from painting he enjoys climbing mountains, collecting advertising ephemera, antiques and blues and R&B records, cinema architecture and playing the guitar. He recently married Frankie, the girl in the picture.

MEIKLEJOHN ILLUSTRATION was formed in 1970 by Paul and Chris Meiklejohn, and over the years has established a worldwide reputation as one of the leading groups of illustrators in the graphic arts field. They receive commissions largely from advertising, publishing and the entertainments industry, with clients from all over the globe – Australia, South Africa and East Asia as well as all the major European capitals. The twenty-one illustrators whose work appears in this book demonstrate a great diversity of technique and imagination from high-tech airbrush to Rockwell cute, from Lichtenstein pop to Maxfield Parrish romantic.

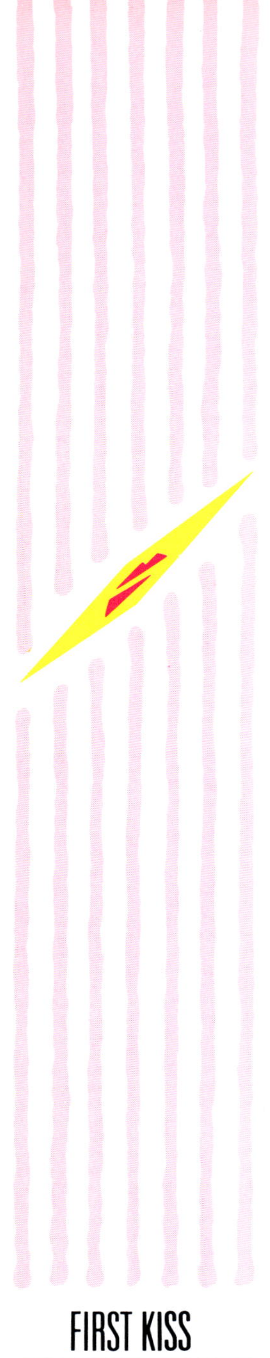

FIRST KISS

PETE KELLY

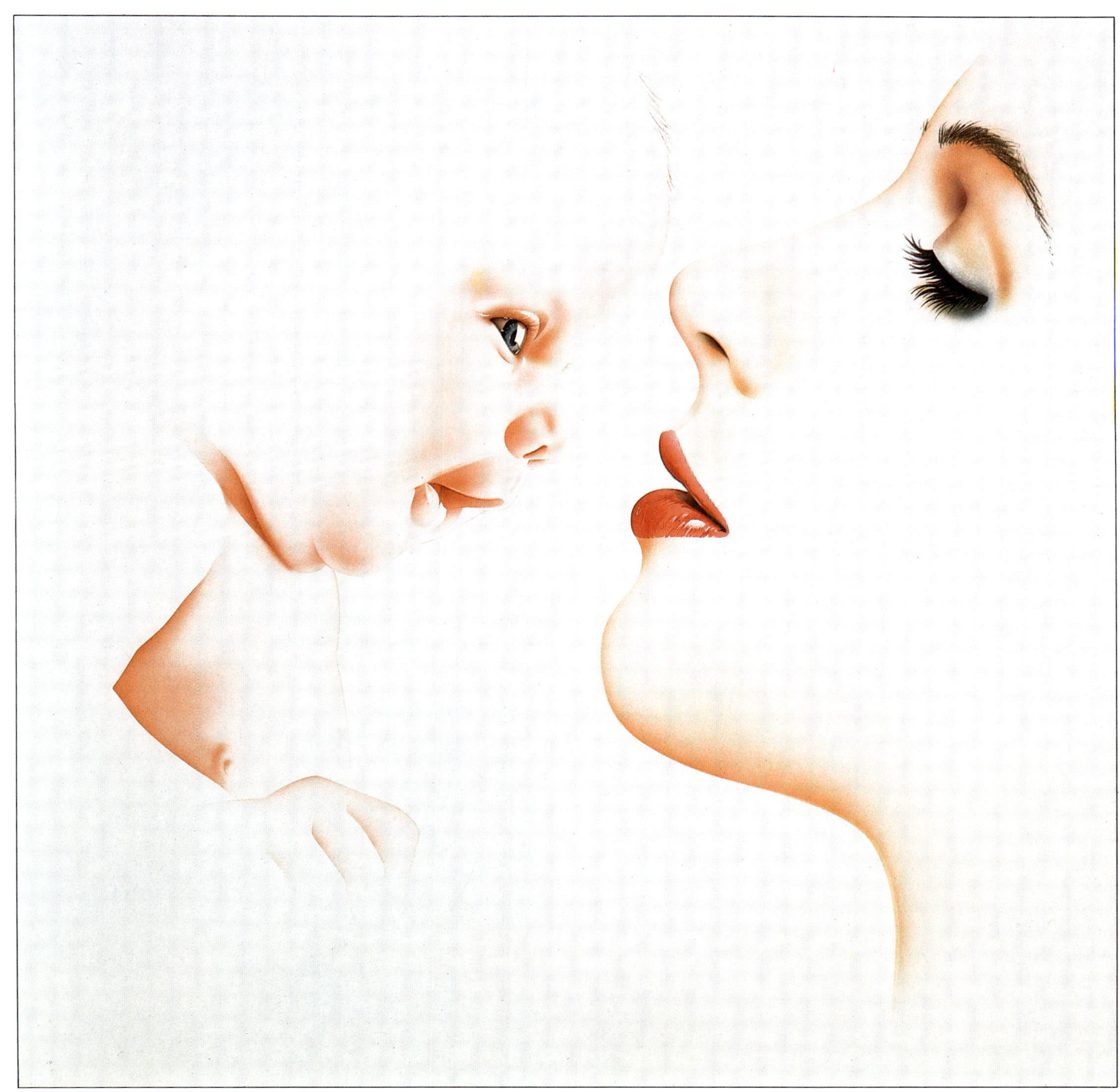

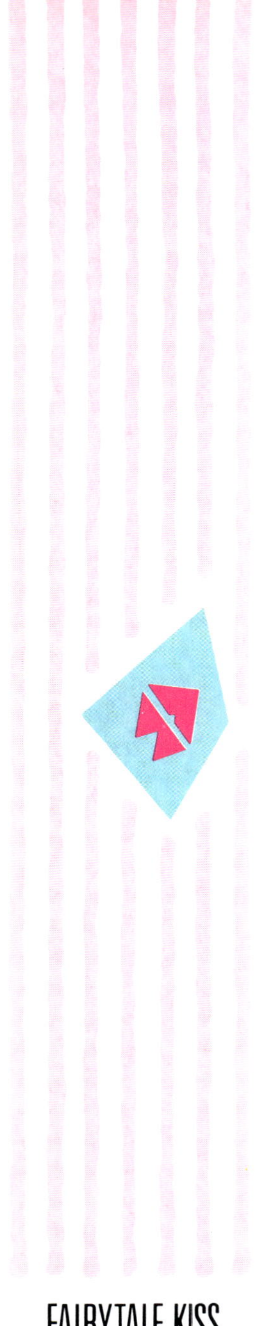

FAIRYTALE KISS

PETER NEAME

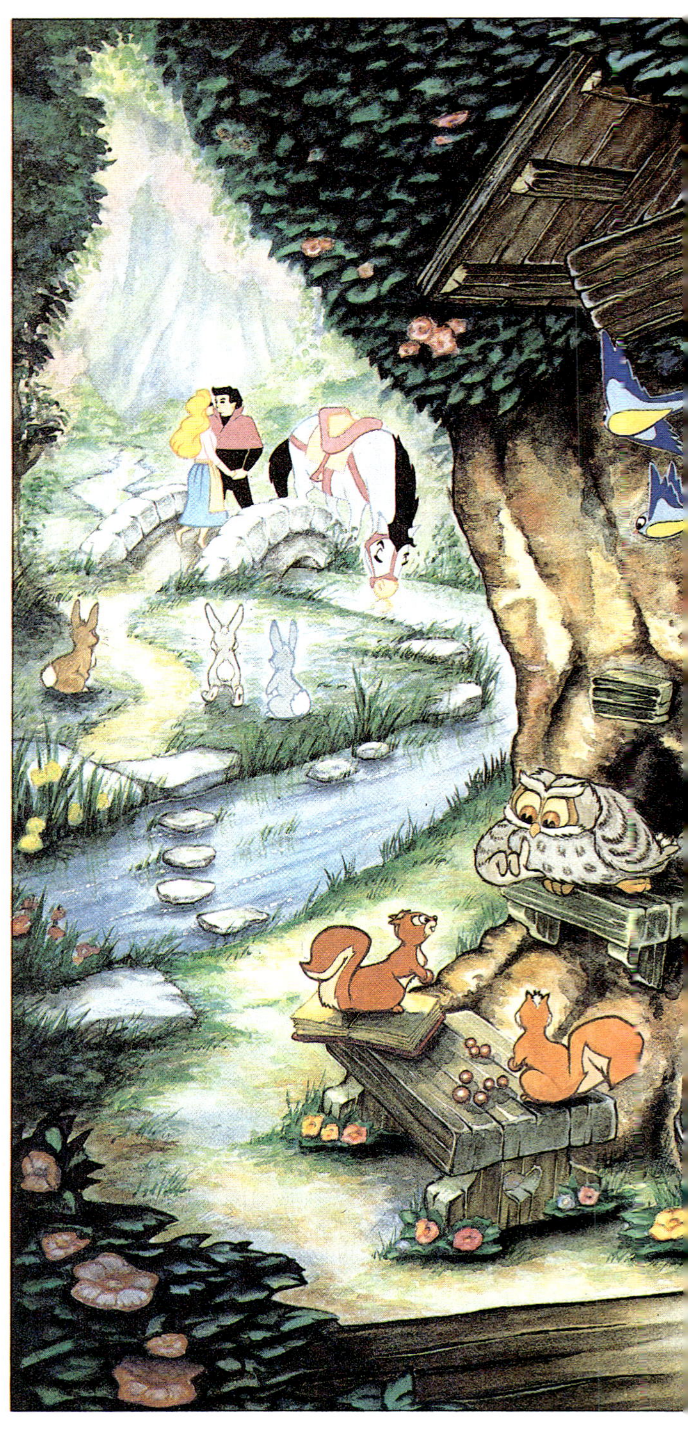

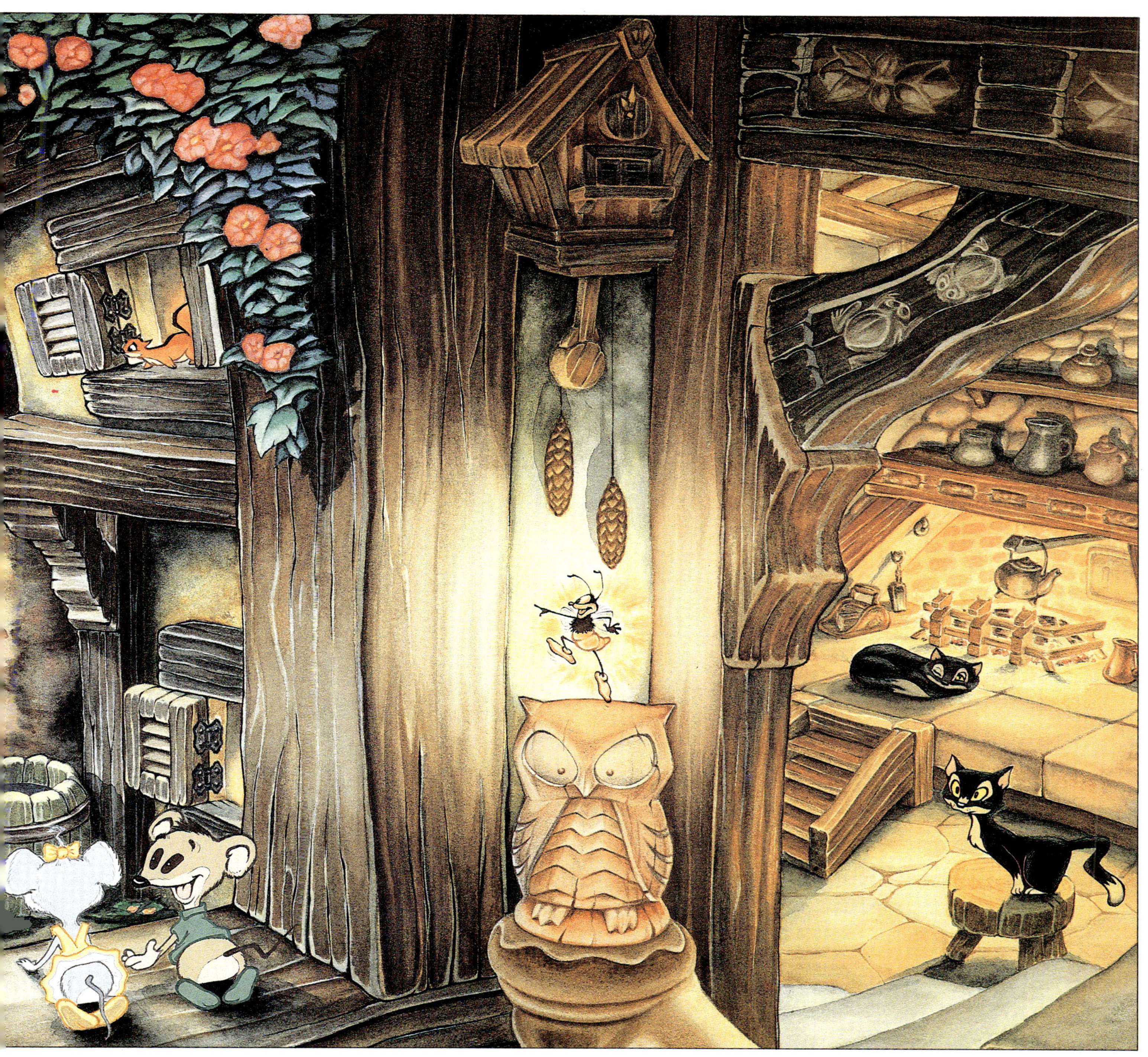

KISSES FOR SALE
MARTIN GASCOIGNE

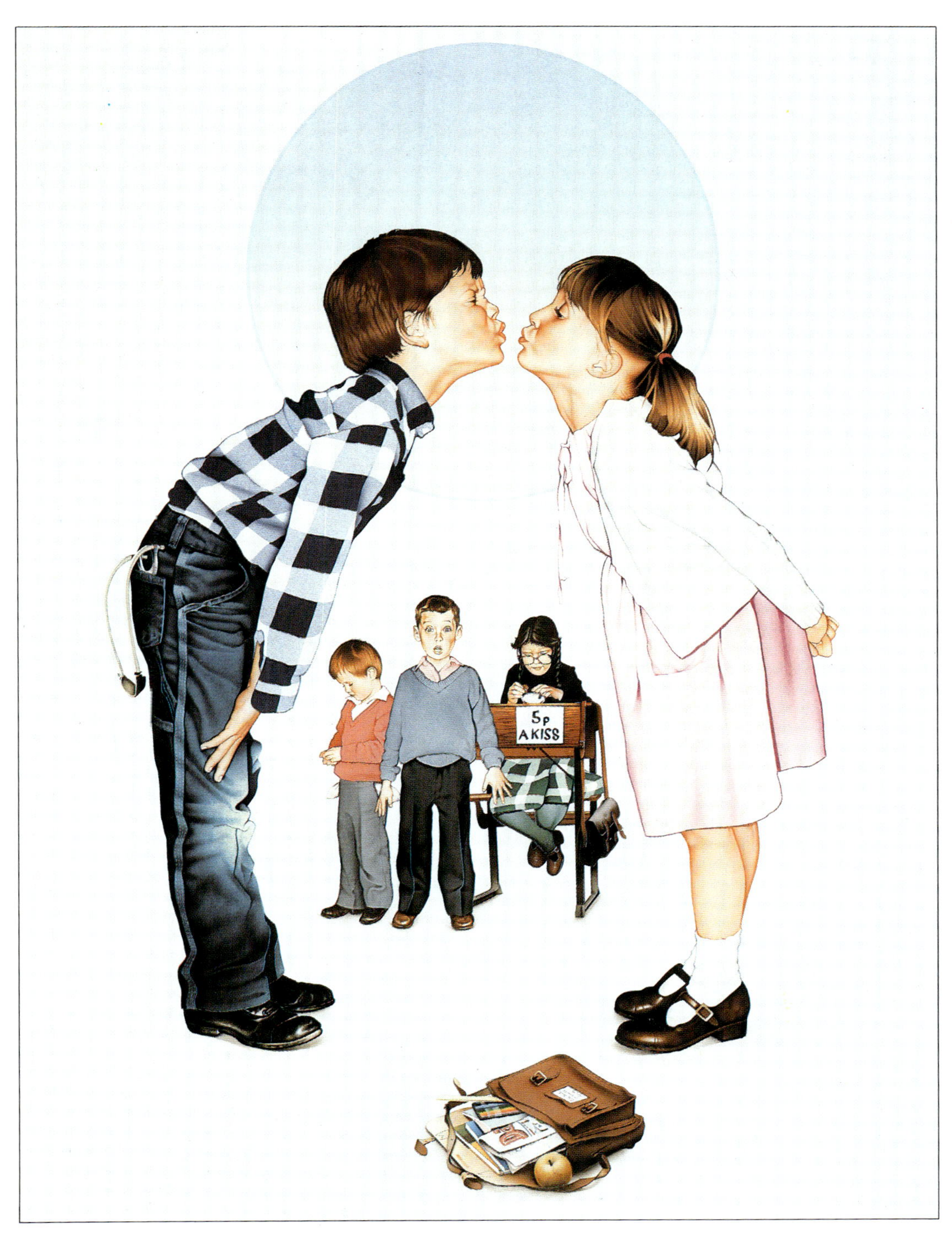
5p
A KISS

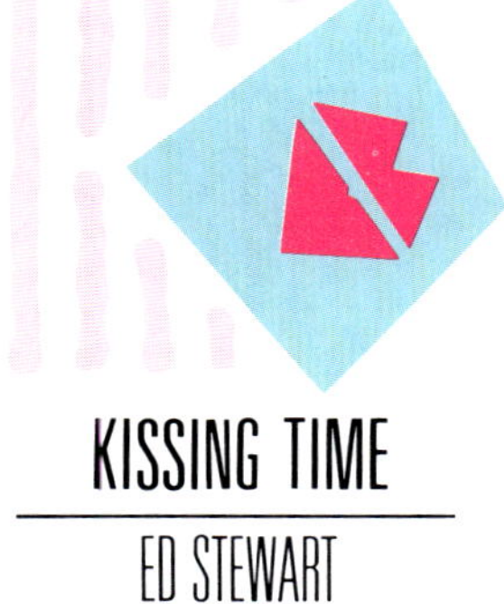

KISSING TIME

ED STEWART

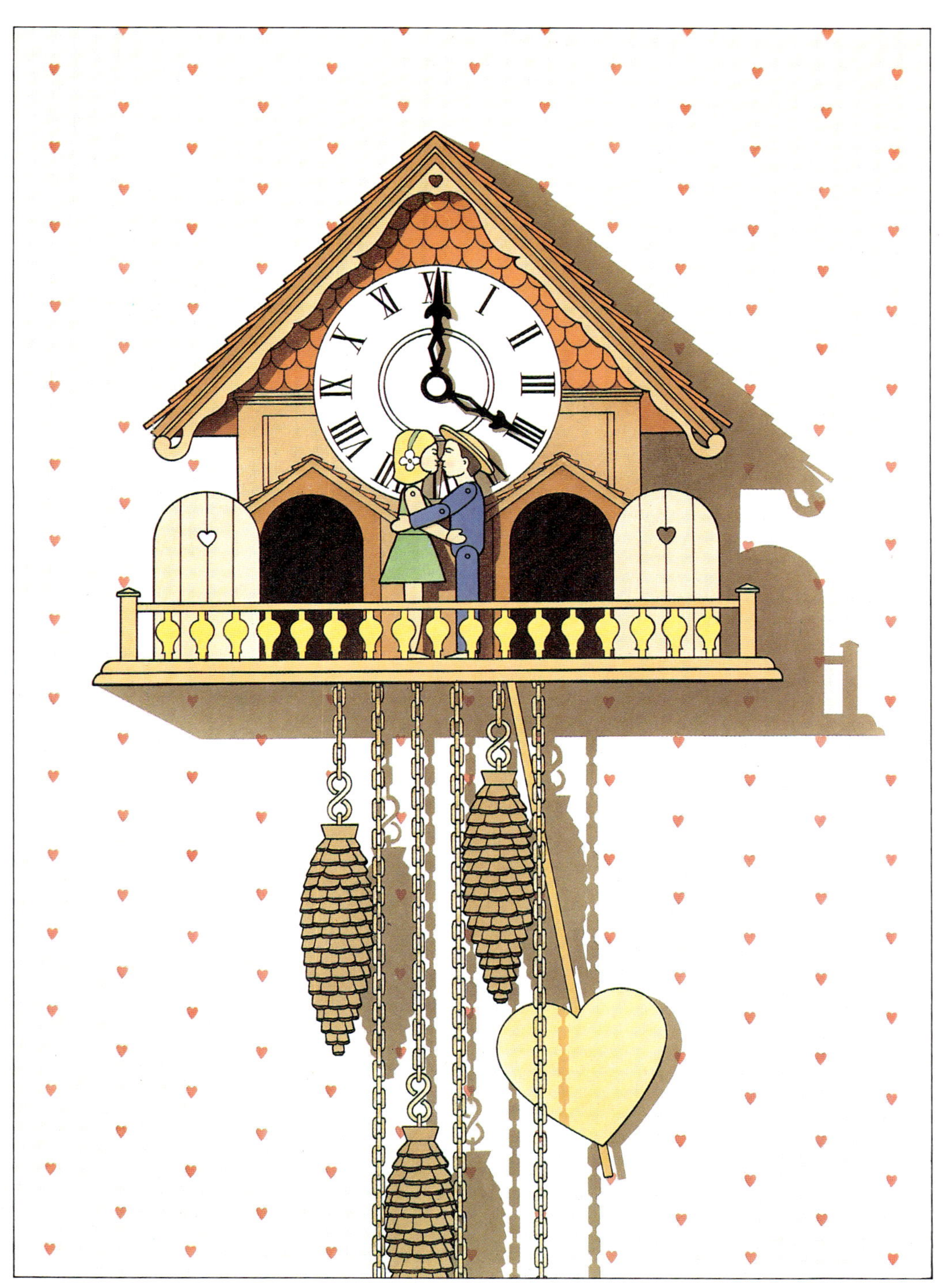

RELUCTANT KISS

DAVID HOLMES

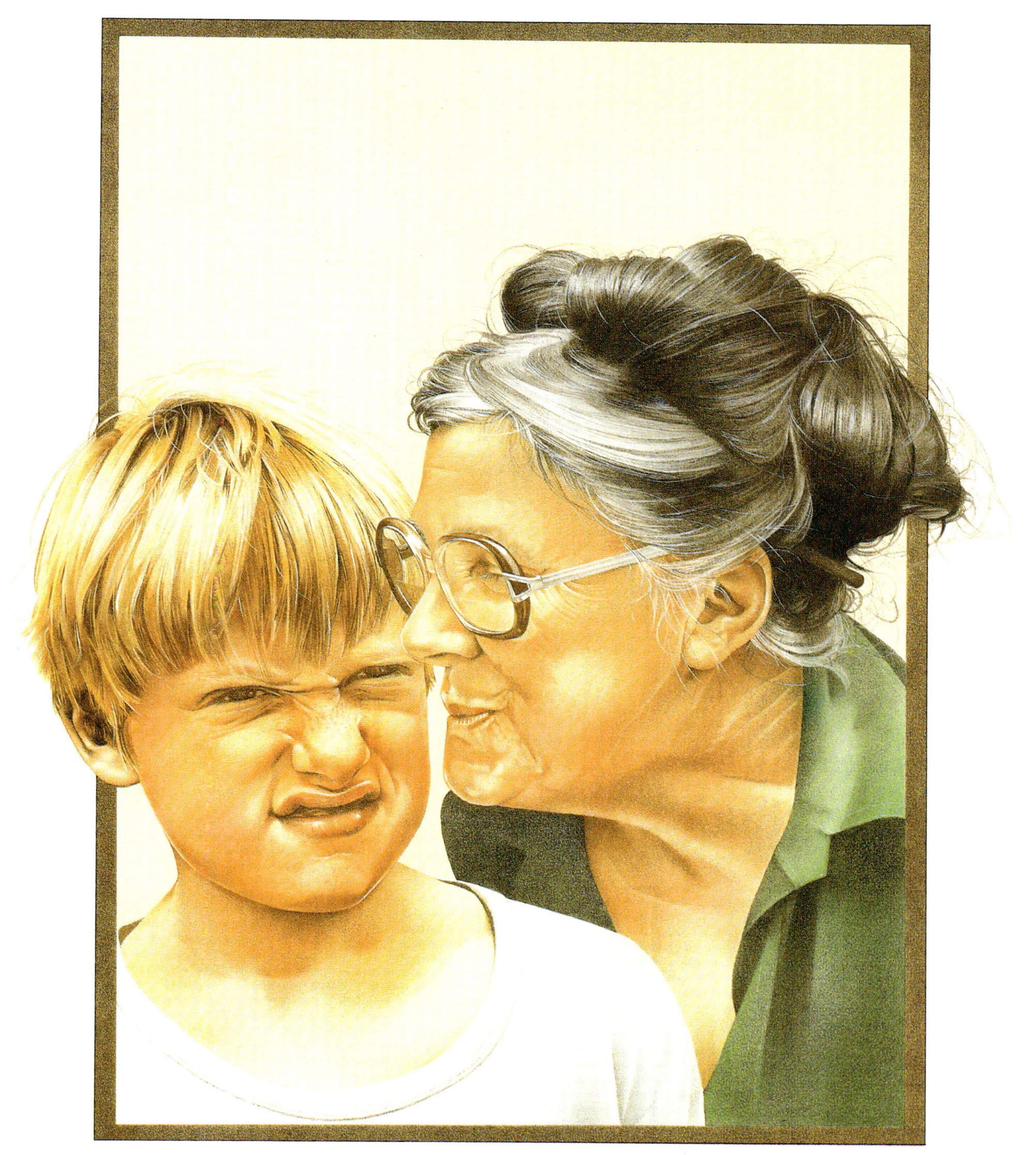

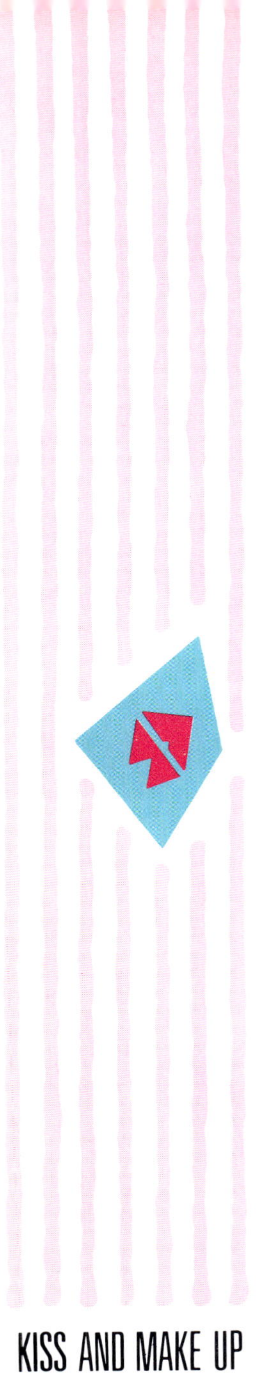

KISS AND MAKE UP

KEITH LABAN

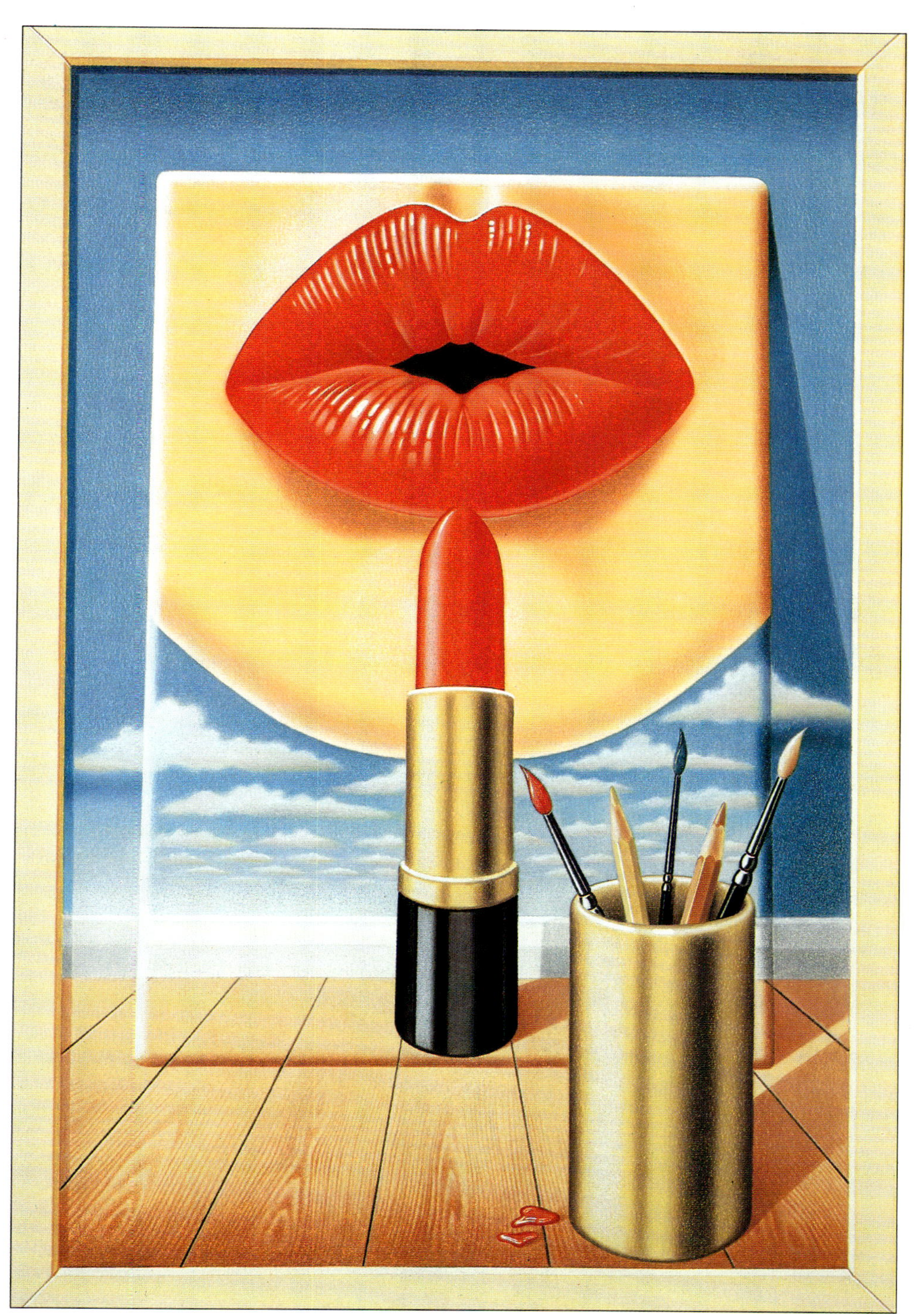

COMIC-STRIP KISS

JOHN MAC

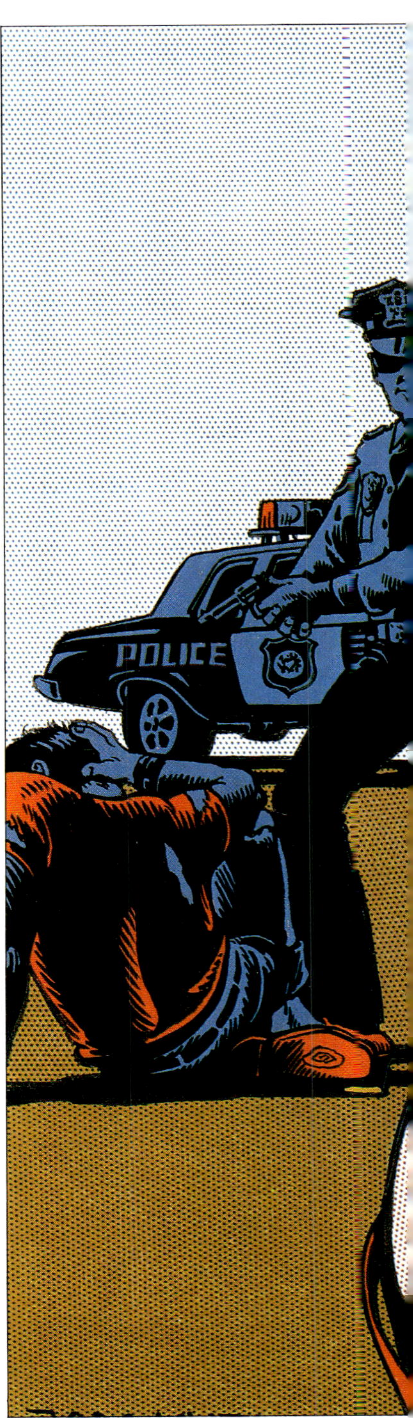

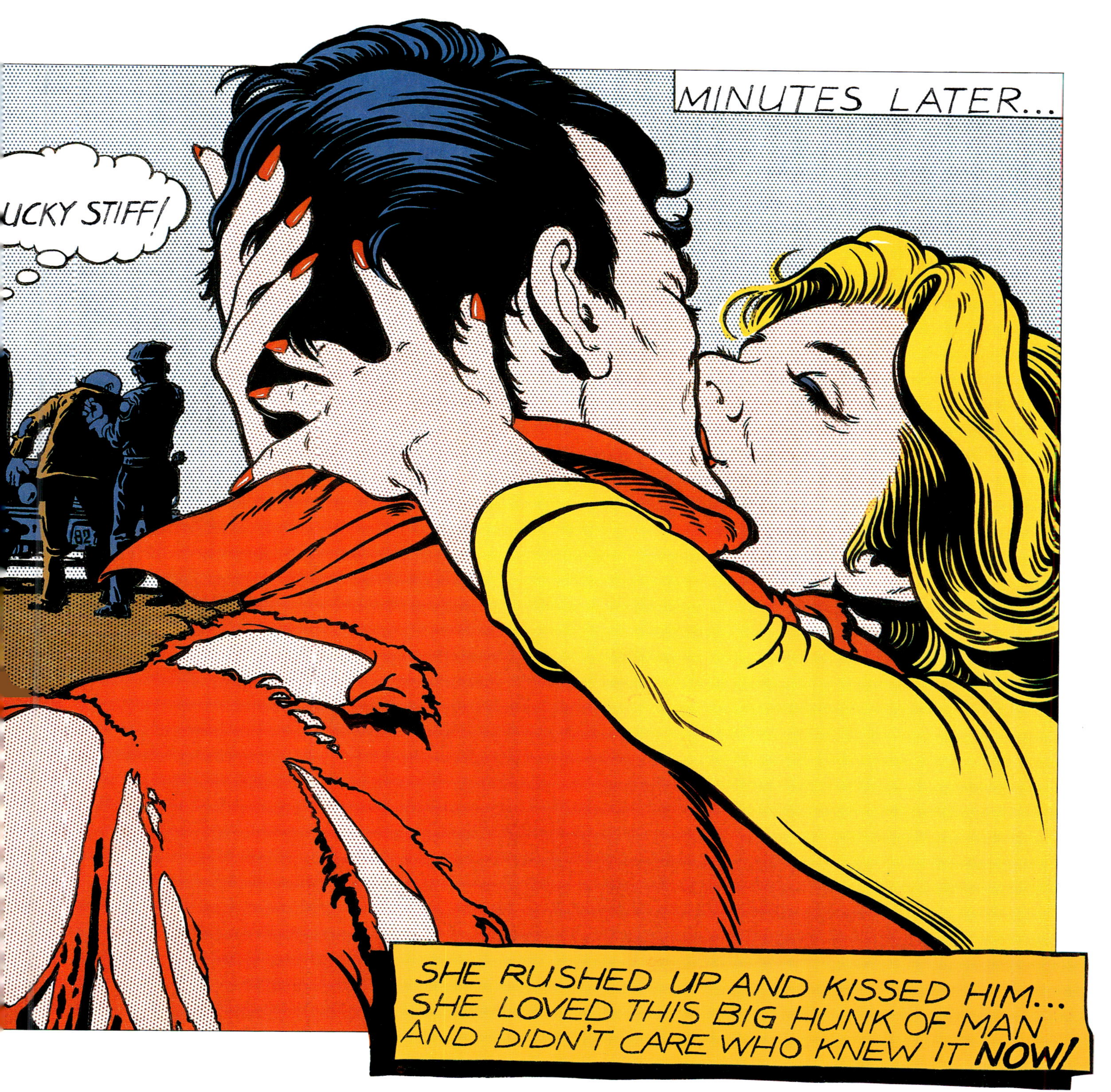
MINUTES LATER...
UCKY STIFF!
SHE RUSHED UP AND KISSED HIM... SHE LOVED THIS BIG HUNK OF MAN AND DIDN'T CARE WHO KNEW IT NOW!

DRIVE-IN KISS

BRIAN JAMES

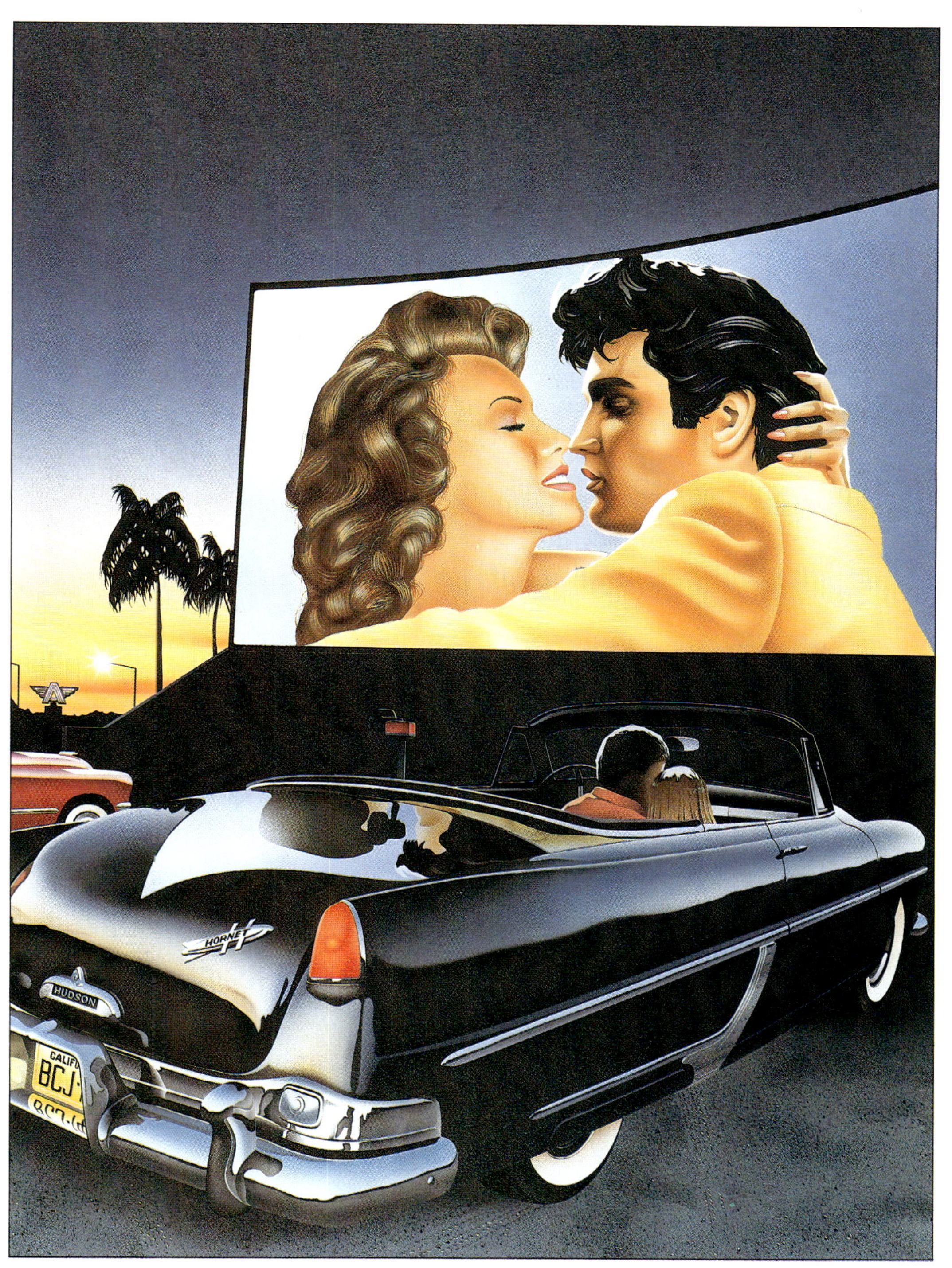
HORNET
HUDSON

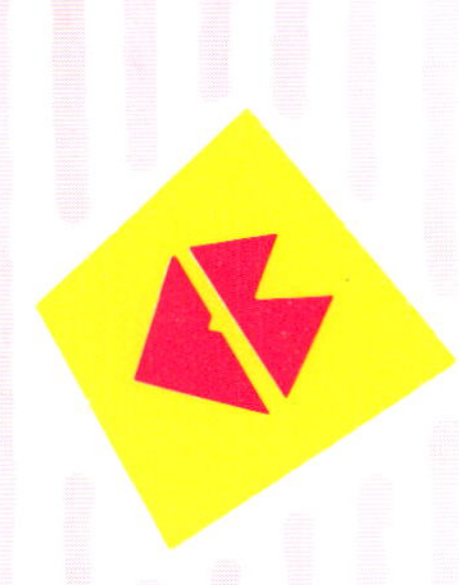

REFLECTIVE KISS

NIGEL TIDMAN

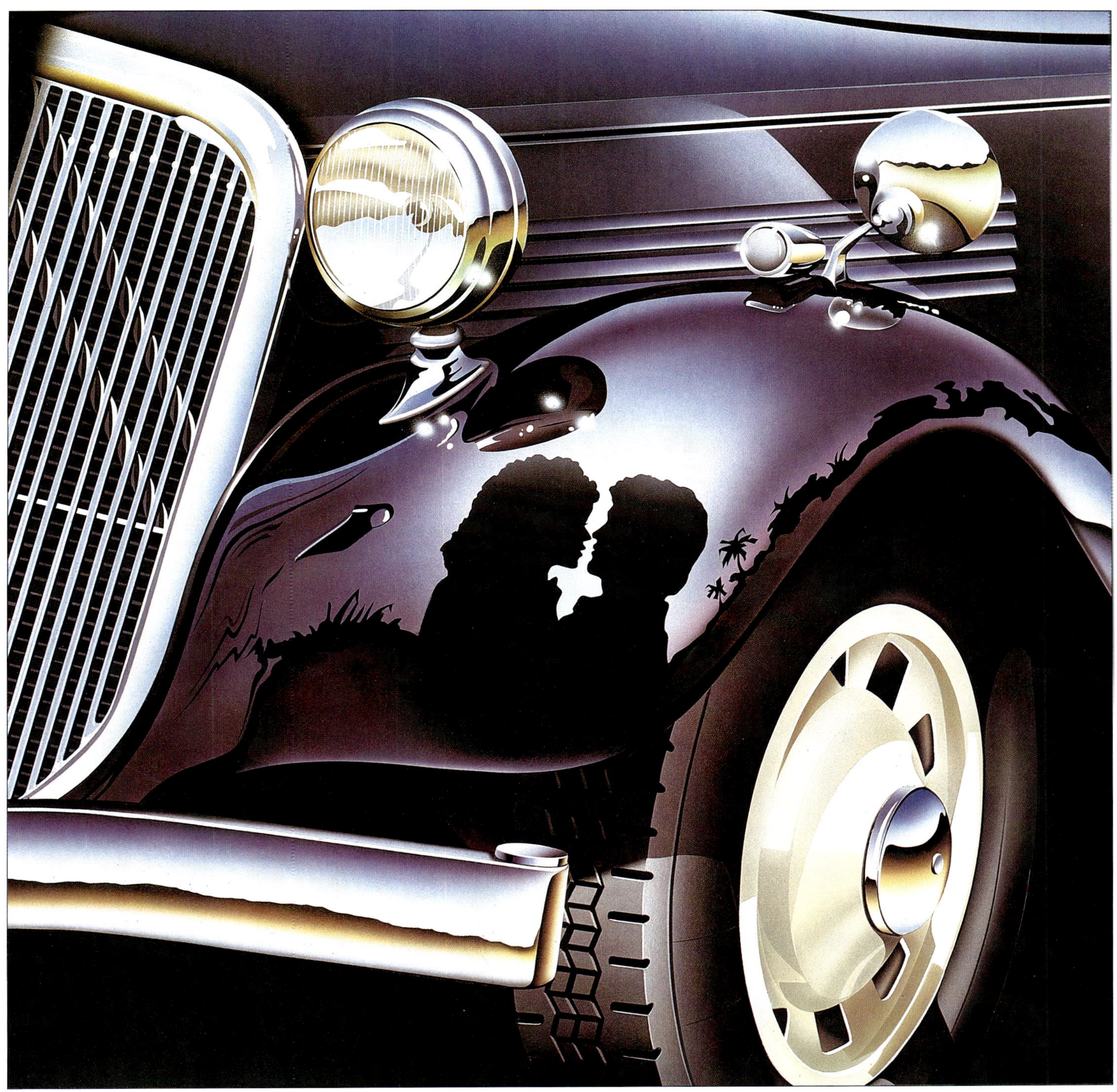

ELECTRIC KISS

SYD BRAK

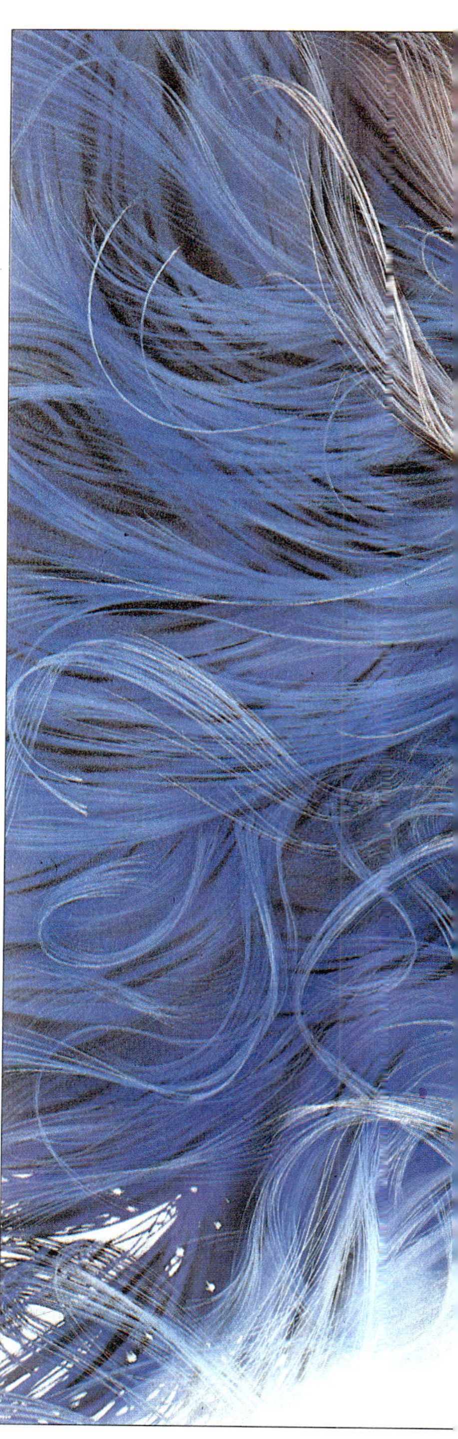

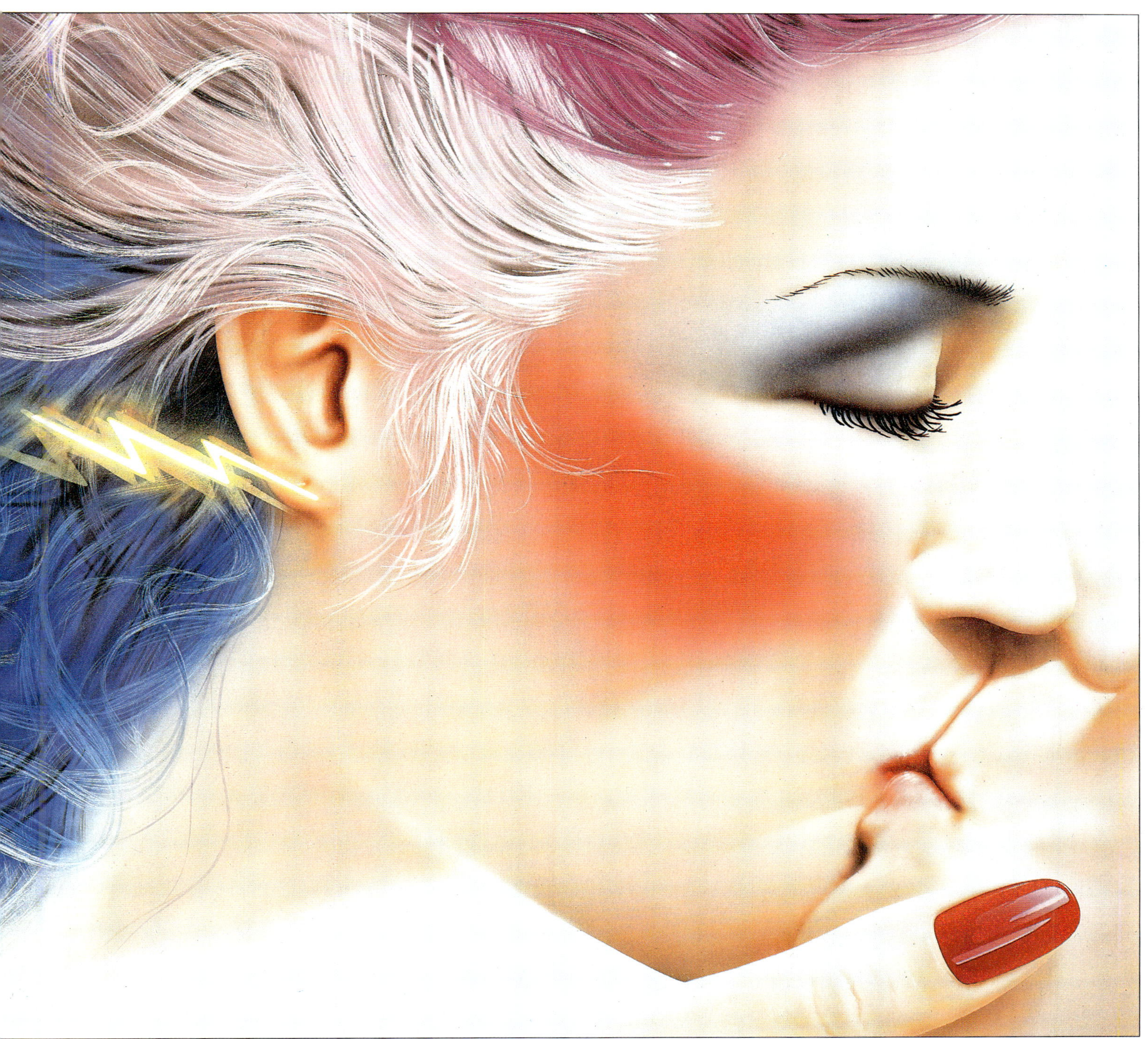

SPORTING KISS

PHIL LITTLER

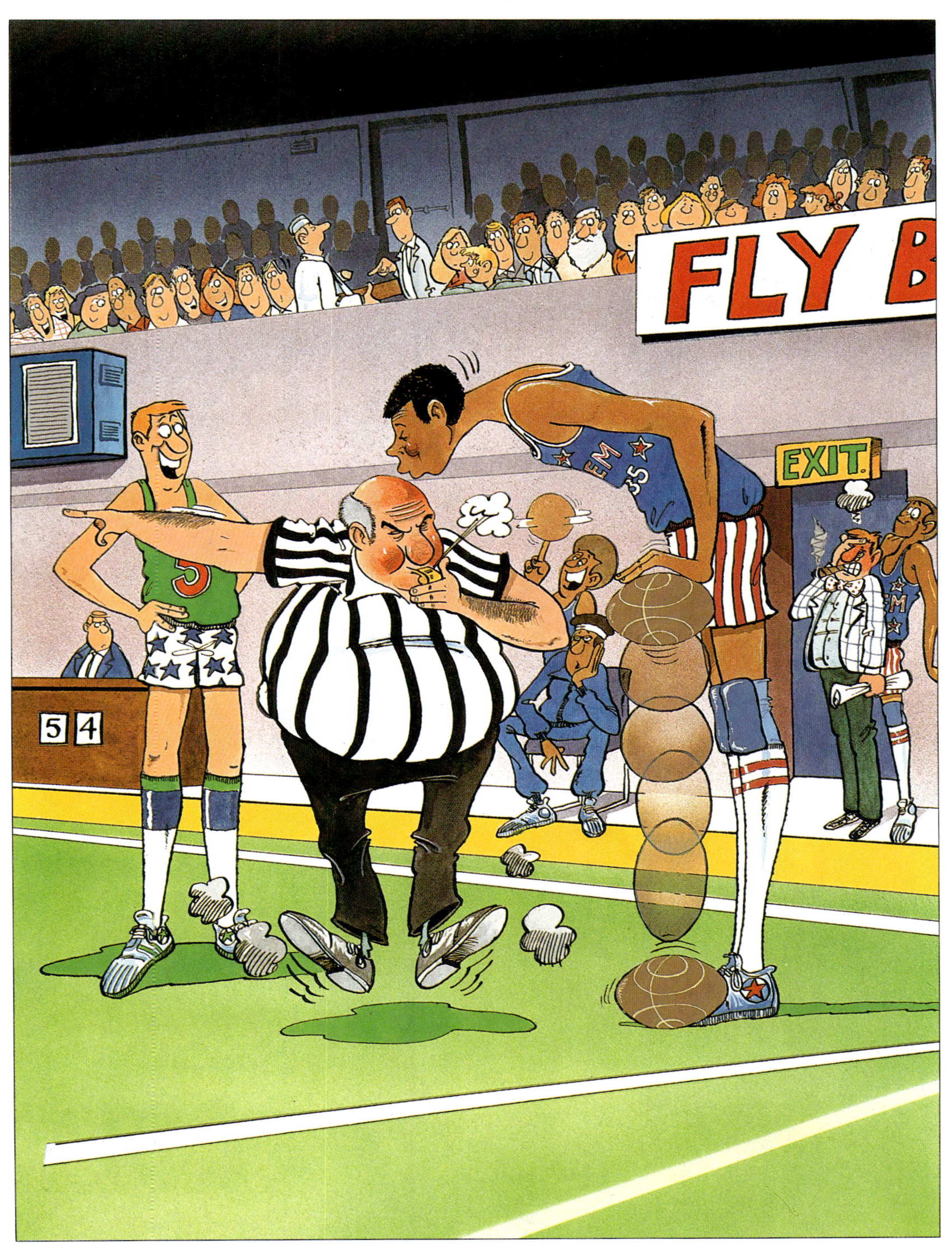
FLY B
EXIT
5 4

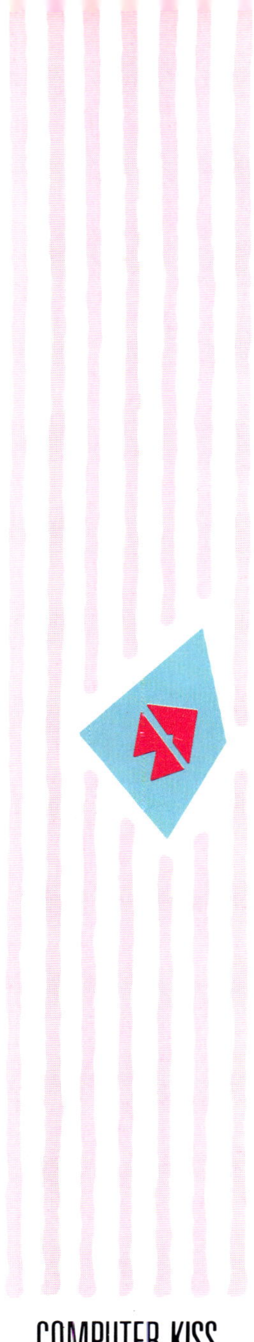

COMPUTER KISS

ED STEWART

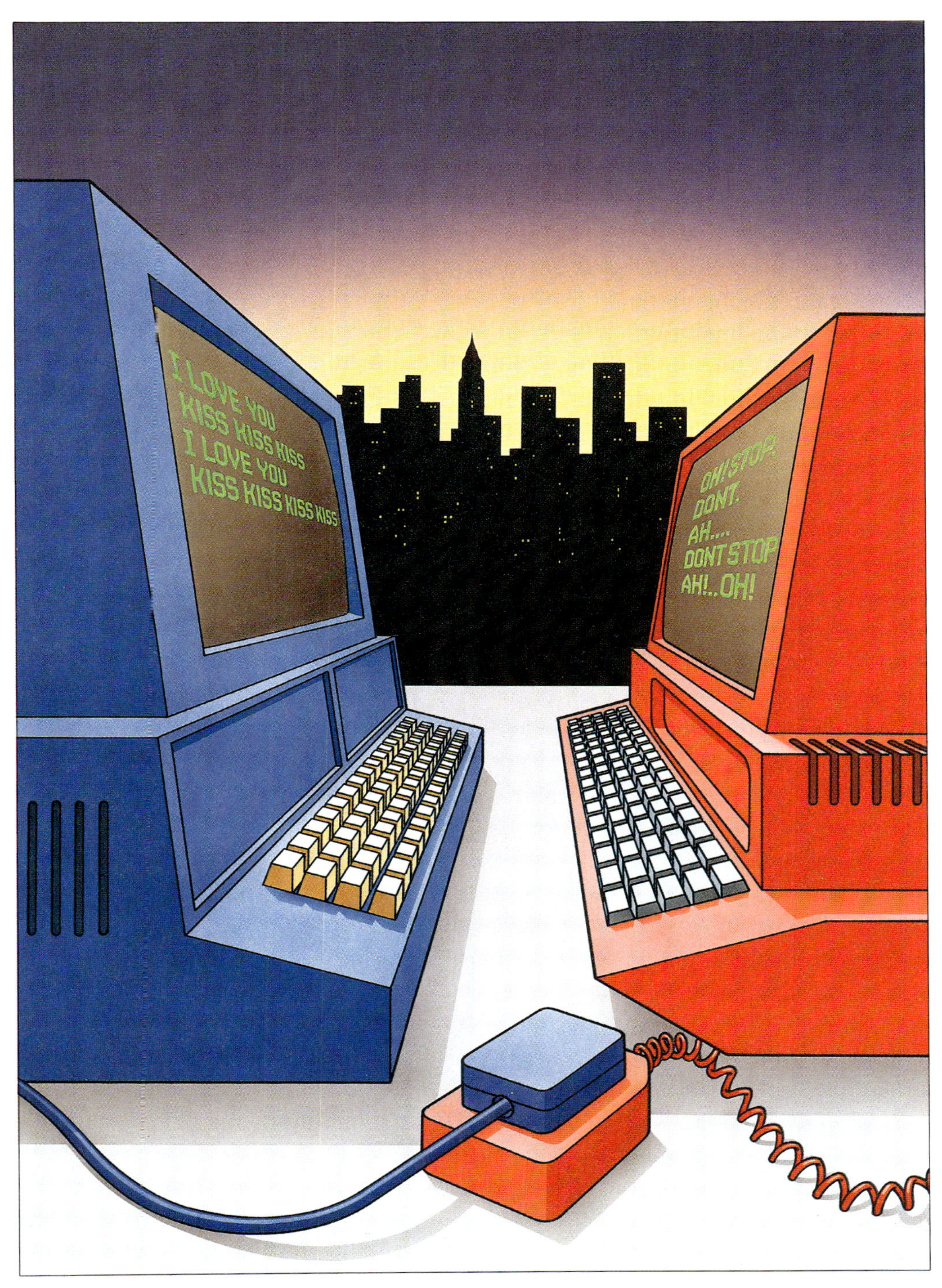
I LOVE YOU
KISS KISS KISS
I LOVE YOU
KISS KISS KISS KISS
OH! STOP.
DONT.
AH....
DONT STOP
AH!..OH!

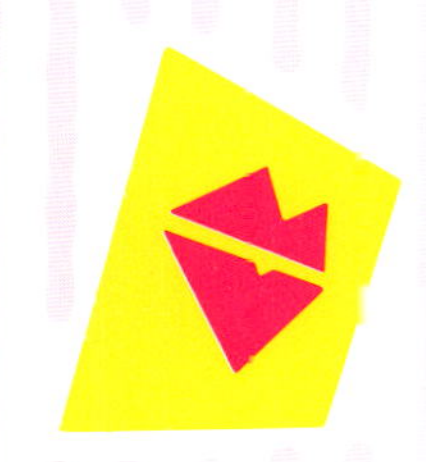

KOOL KATZ KISS

ANDREW FARLEY

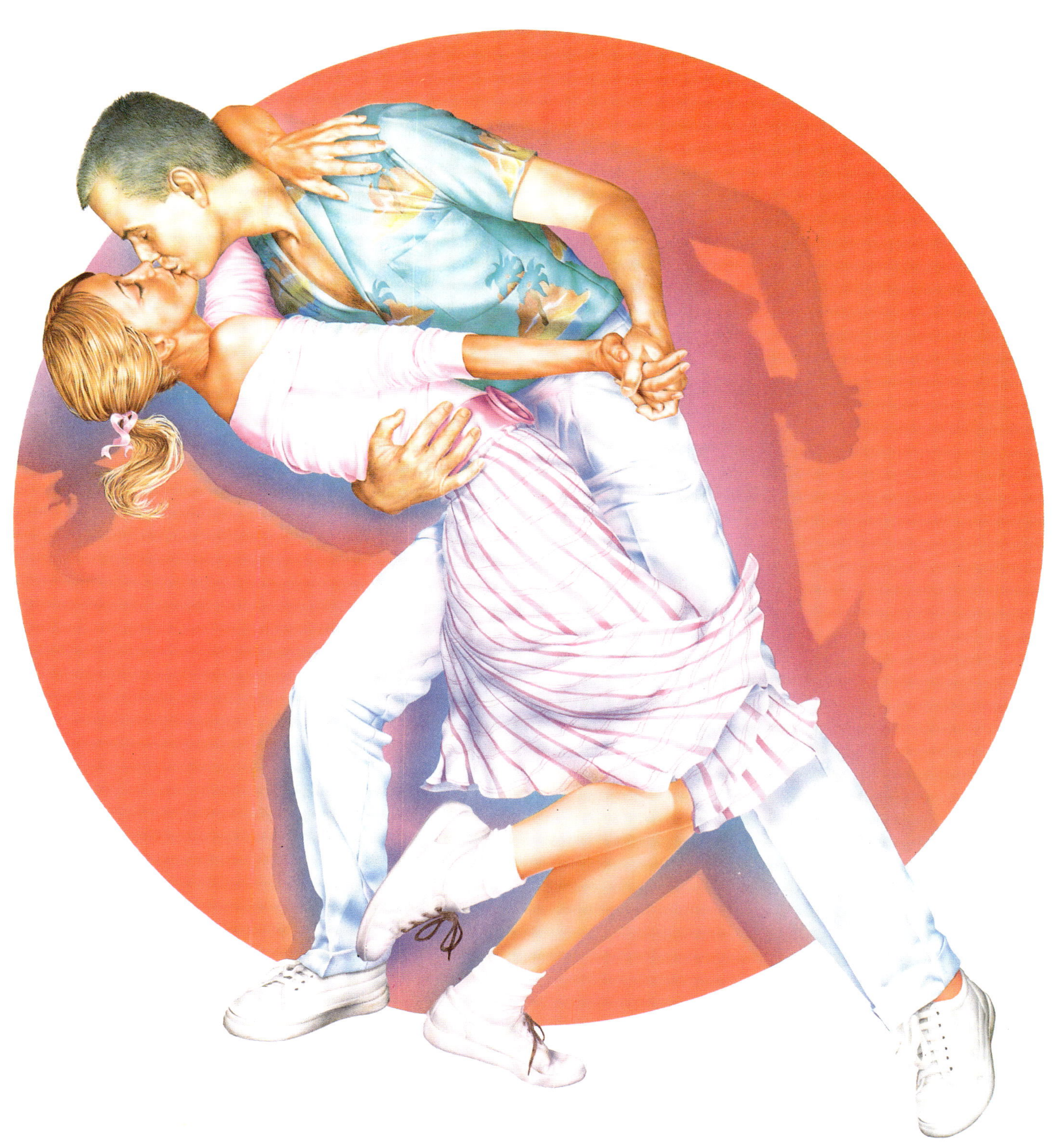

KISS 'N' TELL
BRIAN JAMES

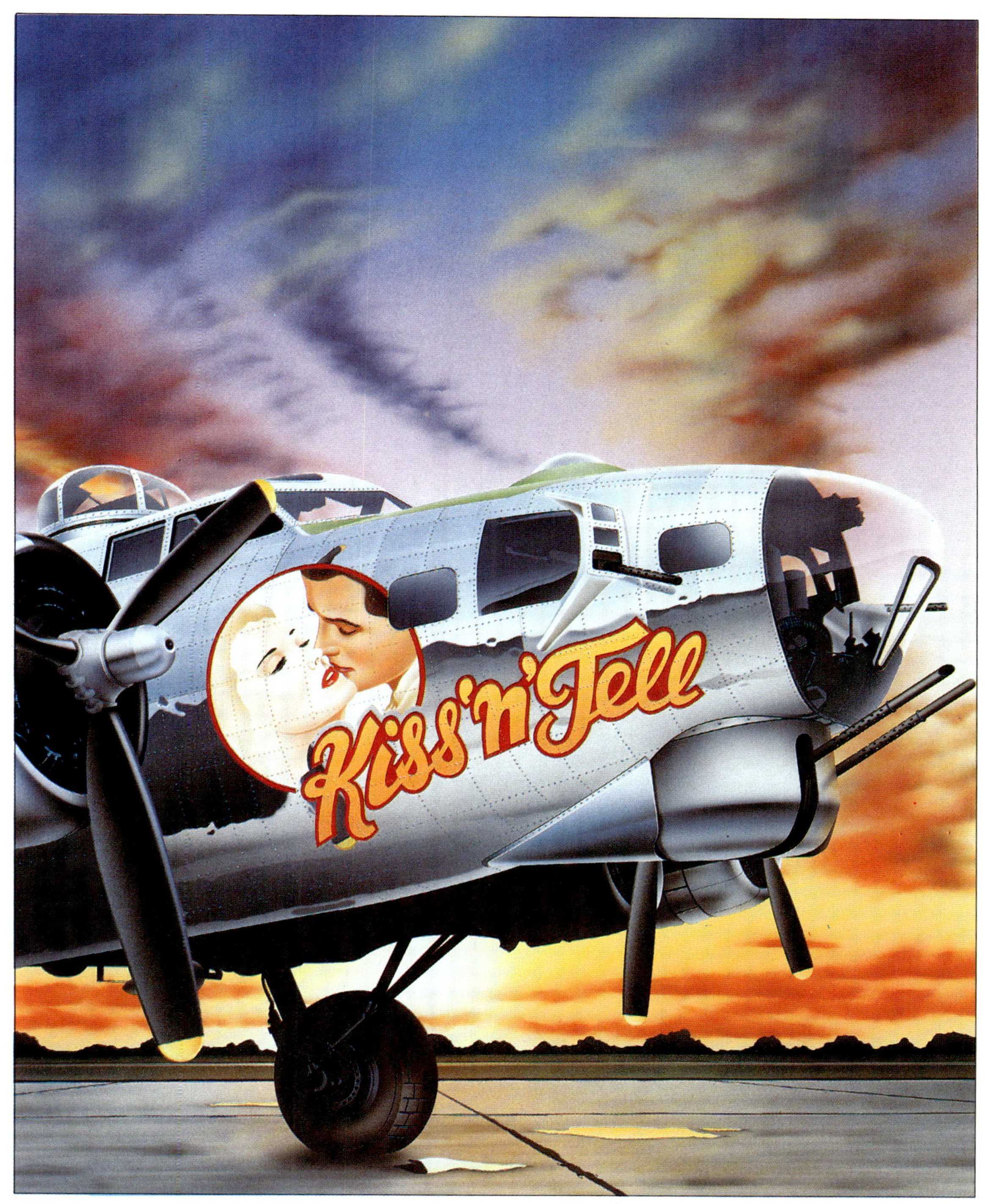
Kiss'n'Tell

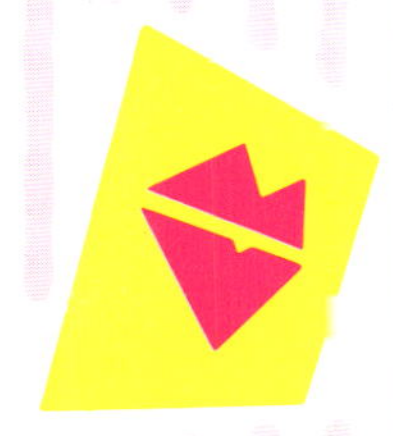

KISS ME KWICK

GAVIN MACLEOD

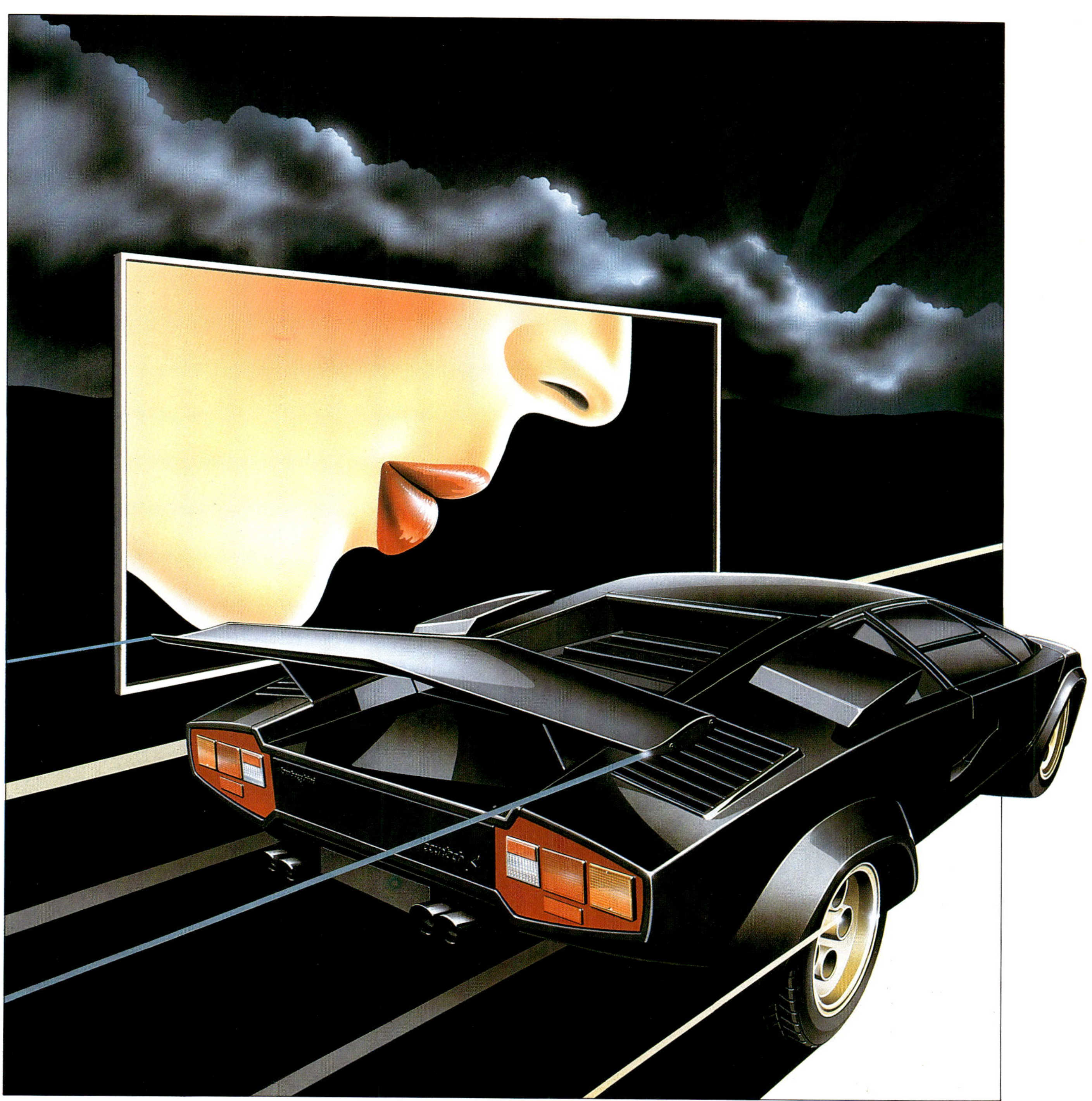

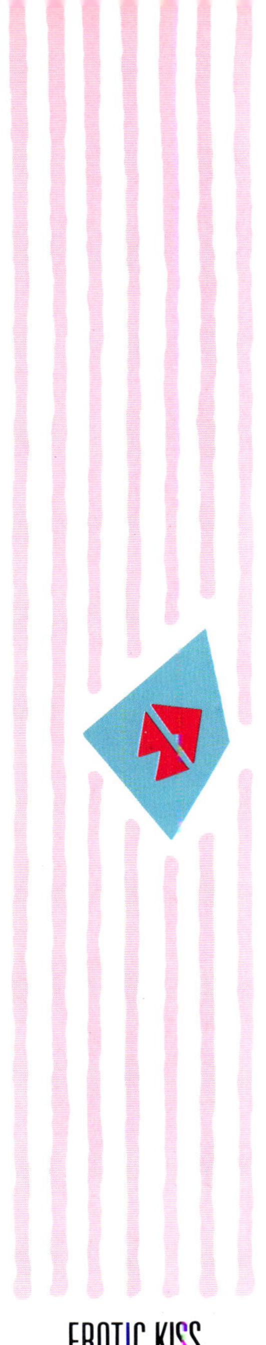

EROTIC KISS

SYD BRAK

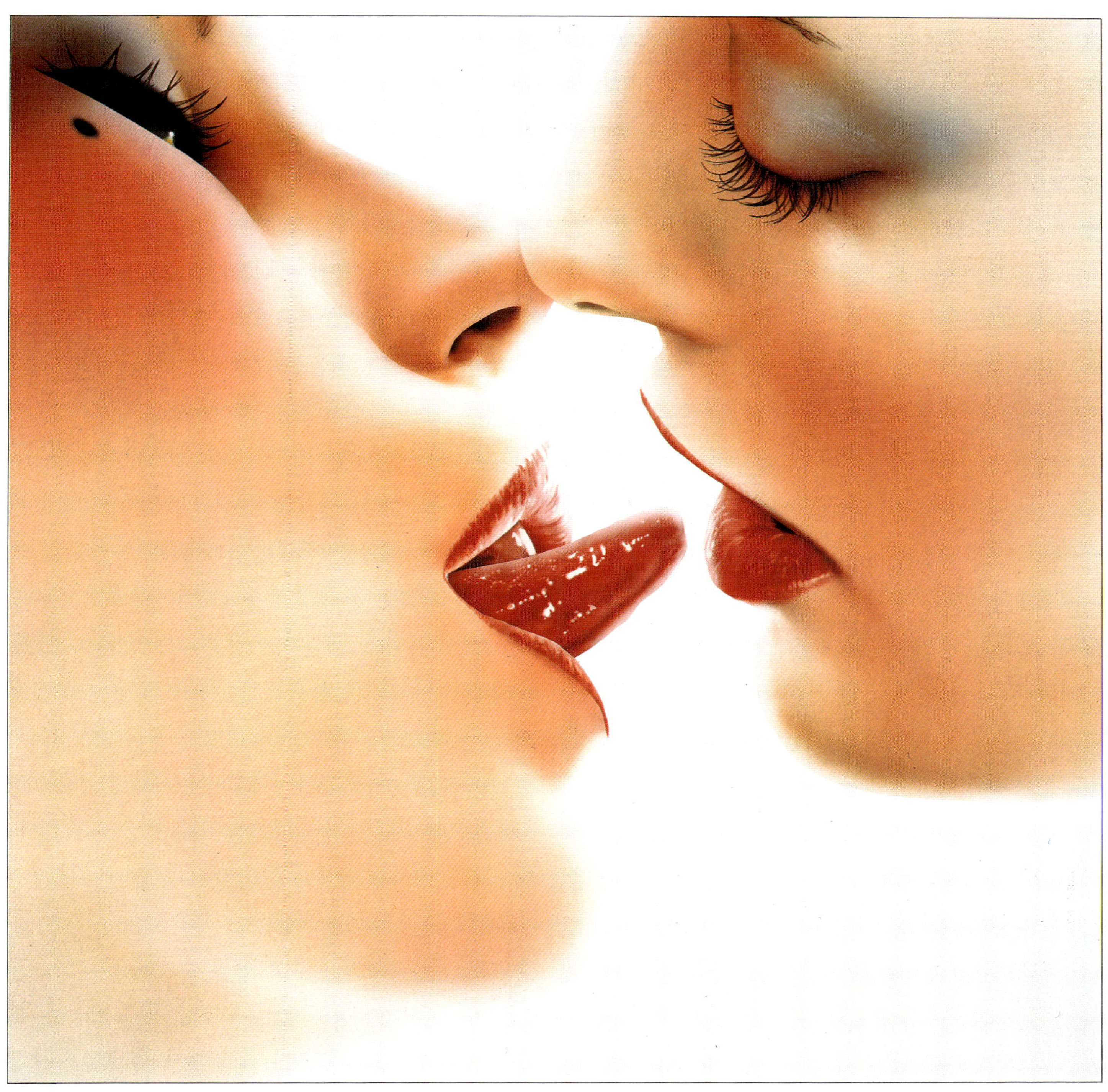

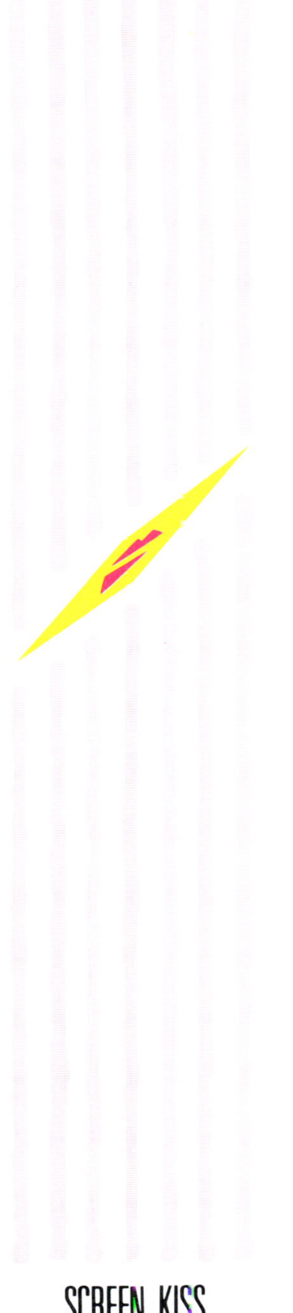

SCREEN KISS

JOHN MAC

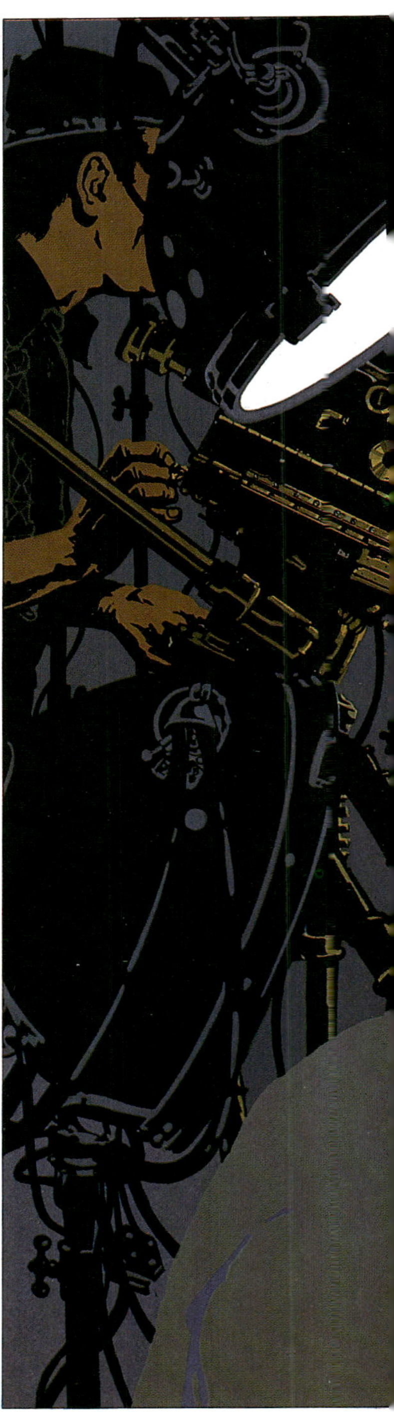

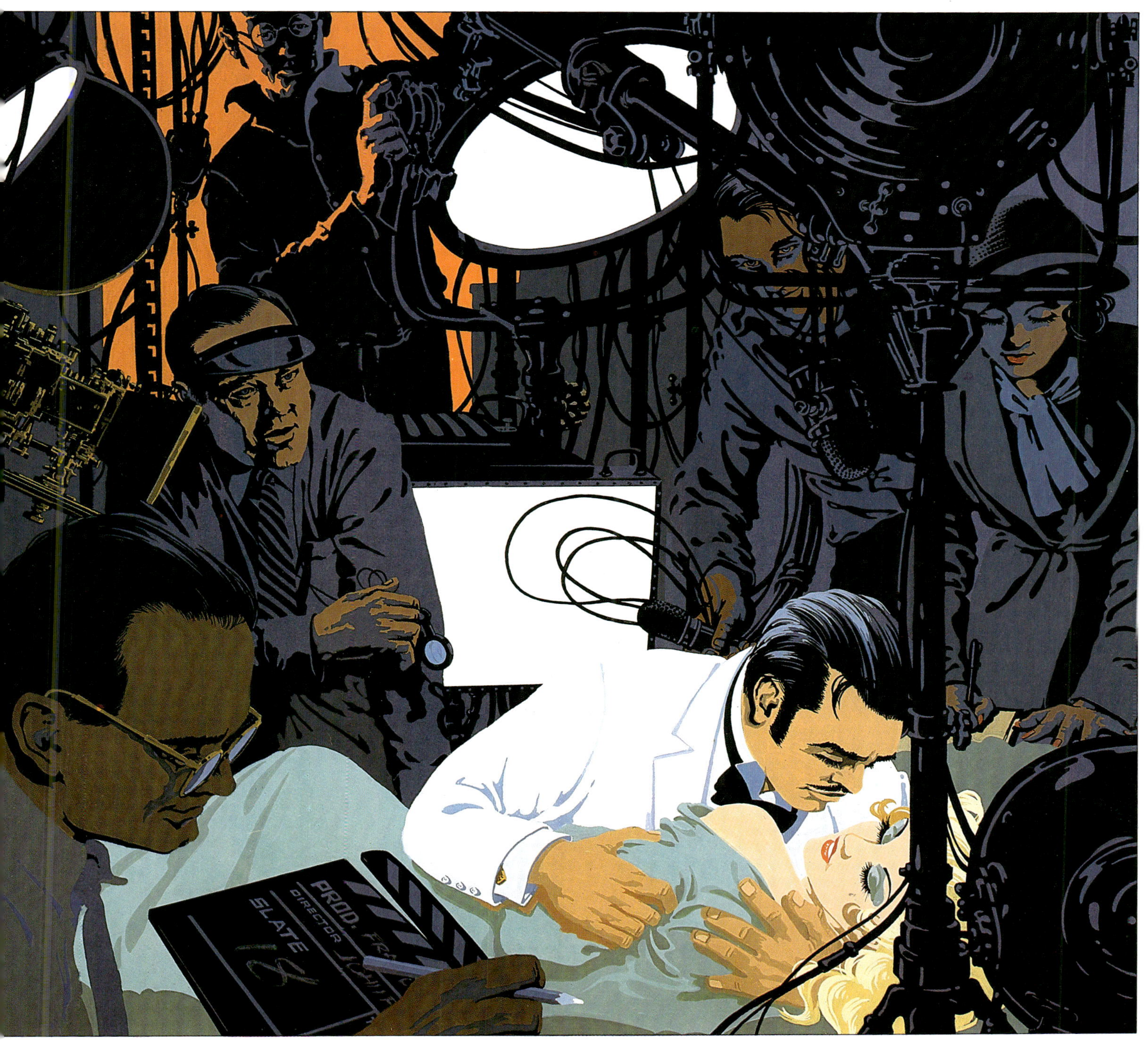
PROD.
DIRECTOR
SLATE

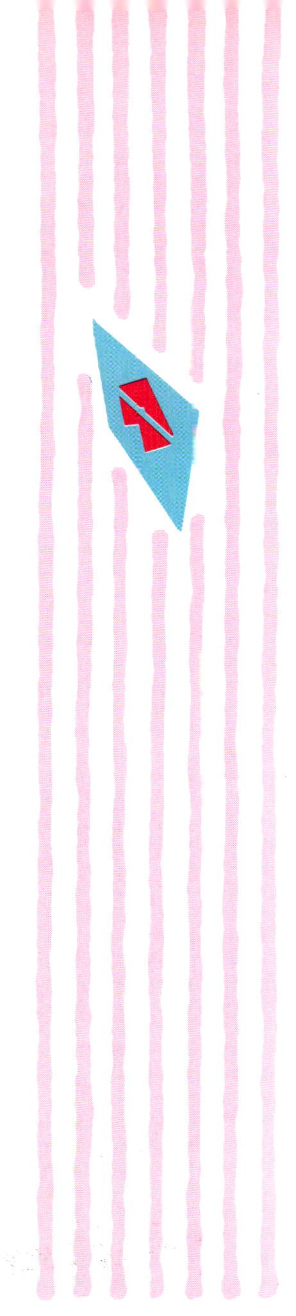

COPYCAT KISS

WARREN MADILL

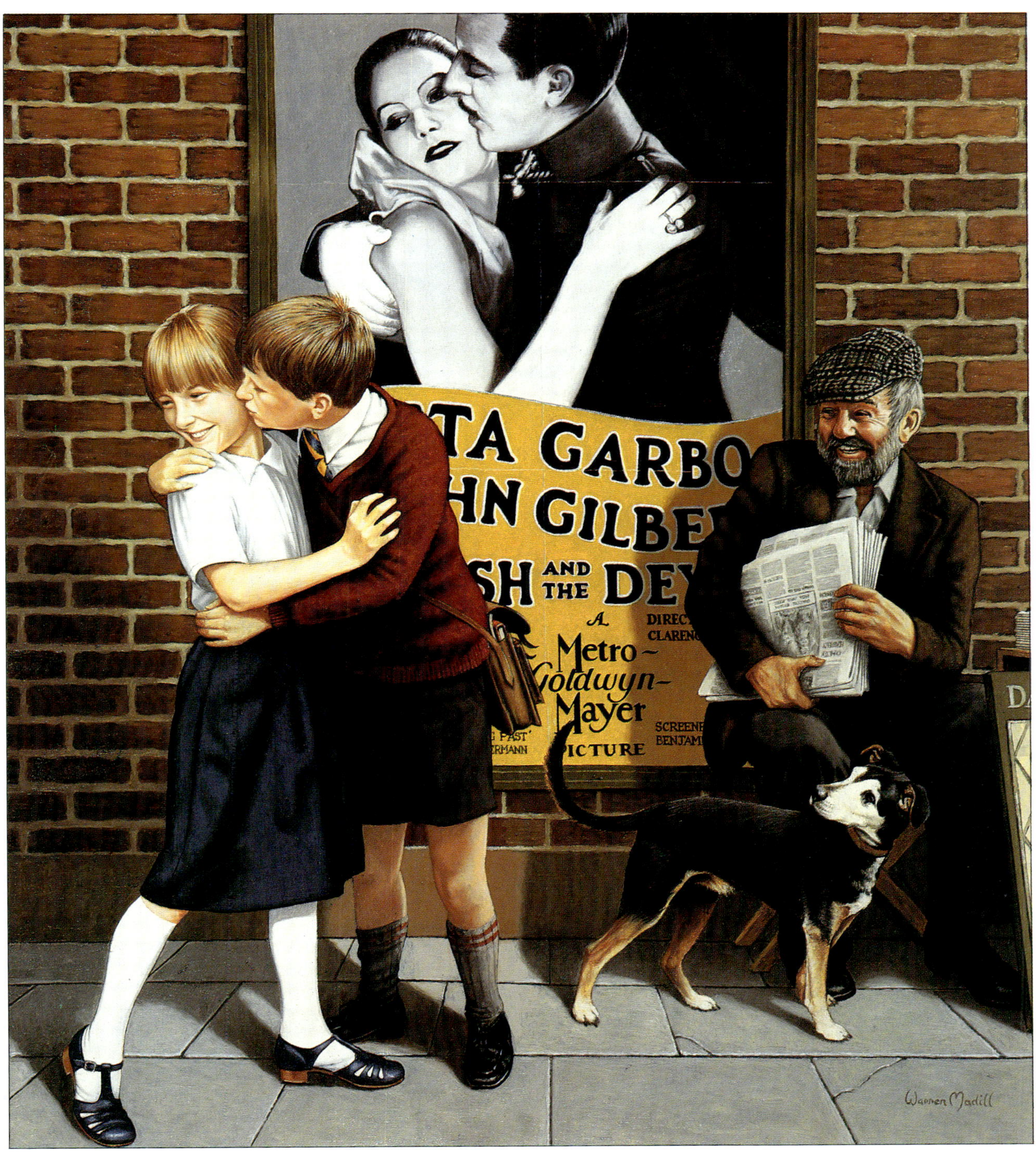

TA GARBO
HN GILBE
SH AND THE DEV
A
Metro-
Goldwyn-
Mayer
PICTURE
Warren Madill

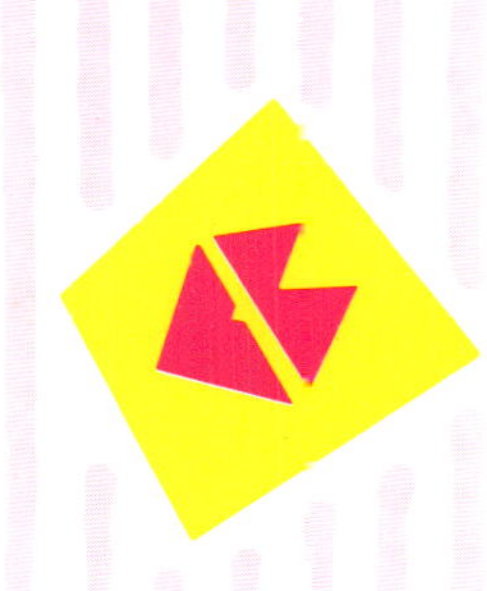

SEDUCTIVE KISS

GARETH WILLIAMS

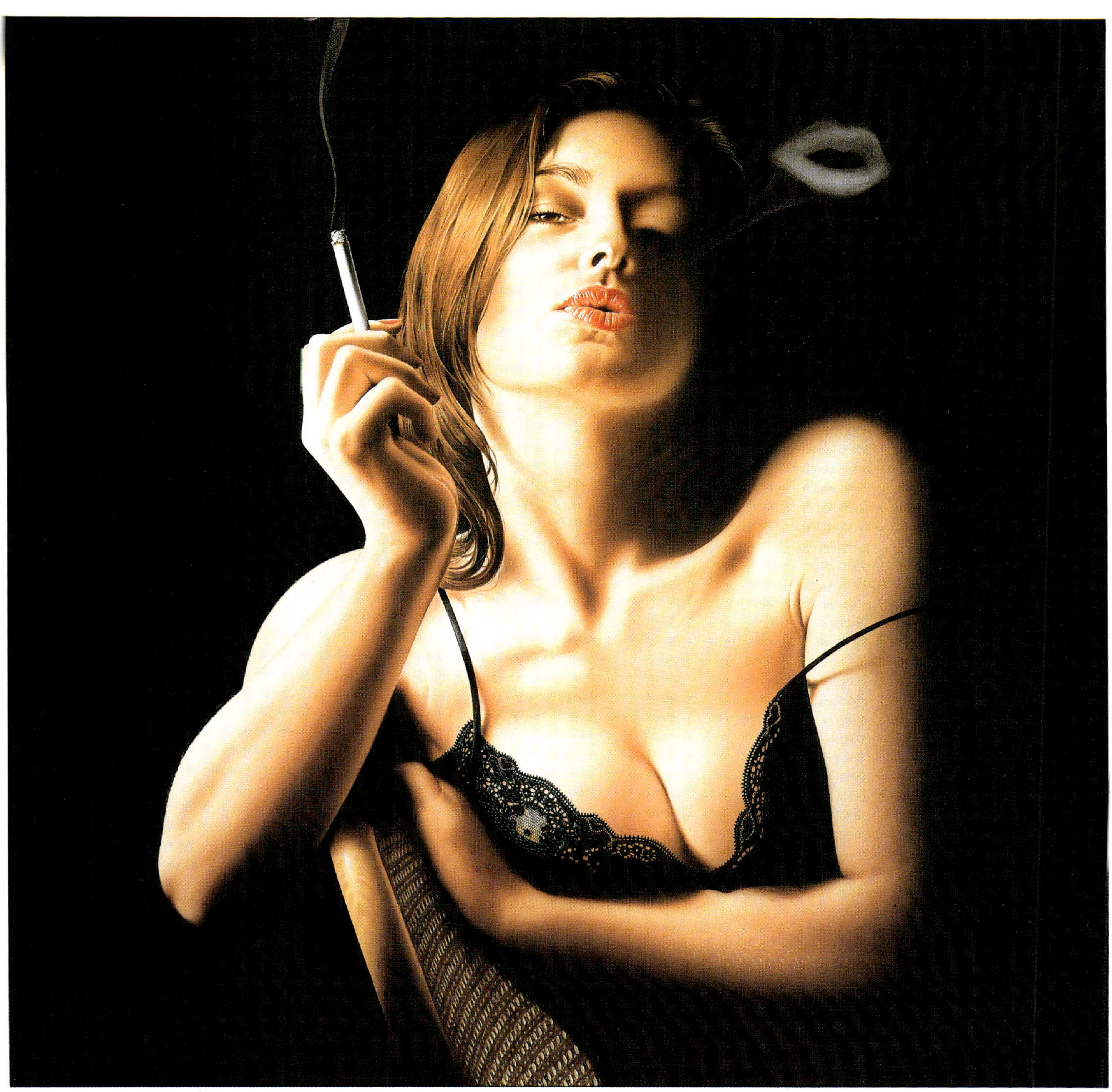

SEALED WITH A KISS
GERRY PRESTON

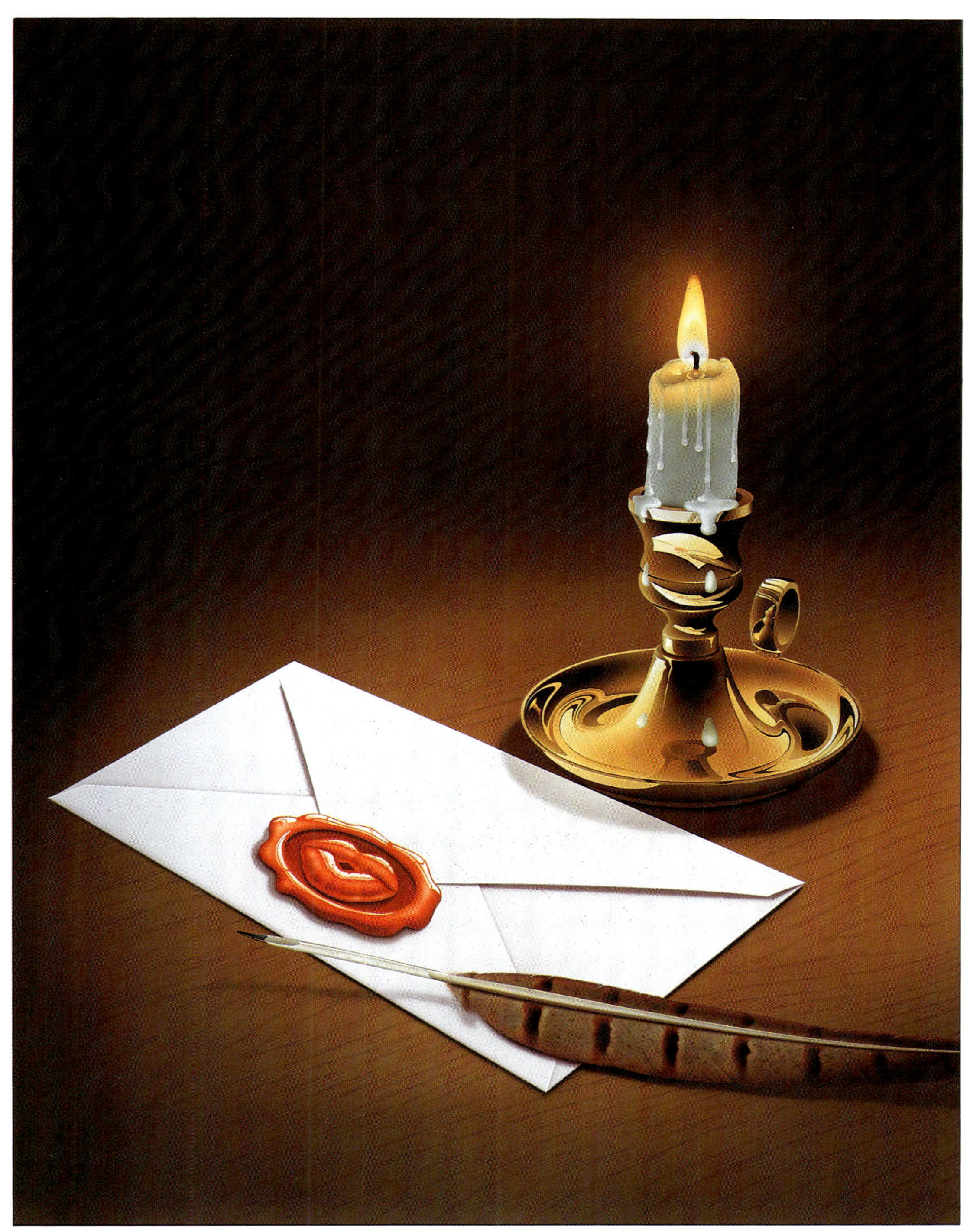

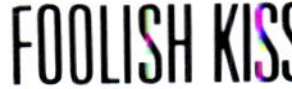

IRVINE PEACOCK

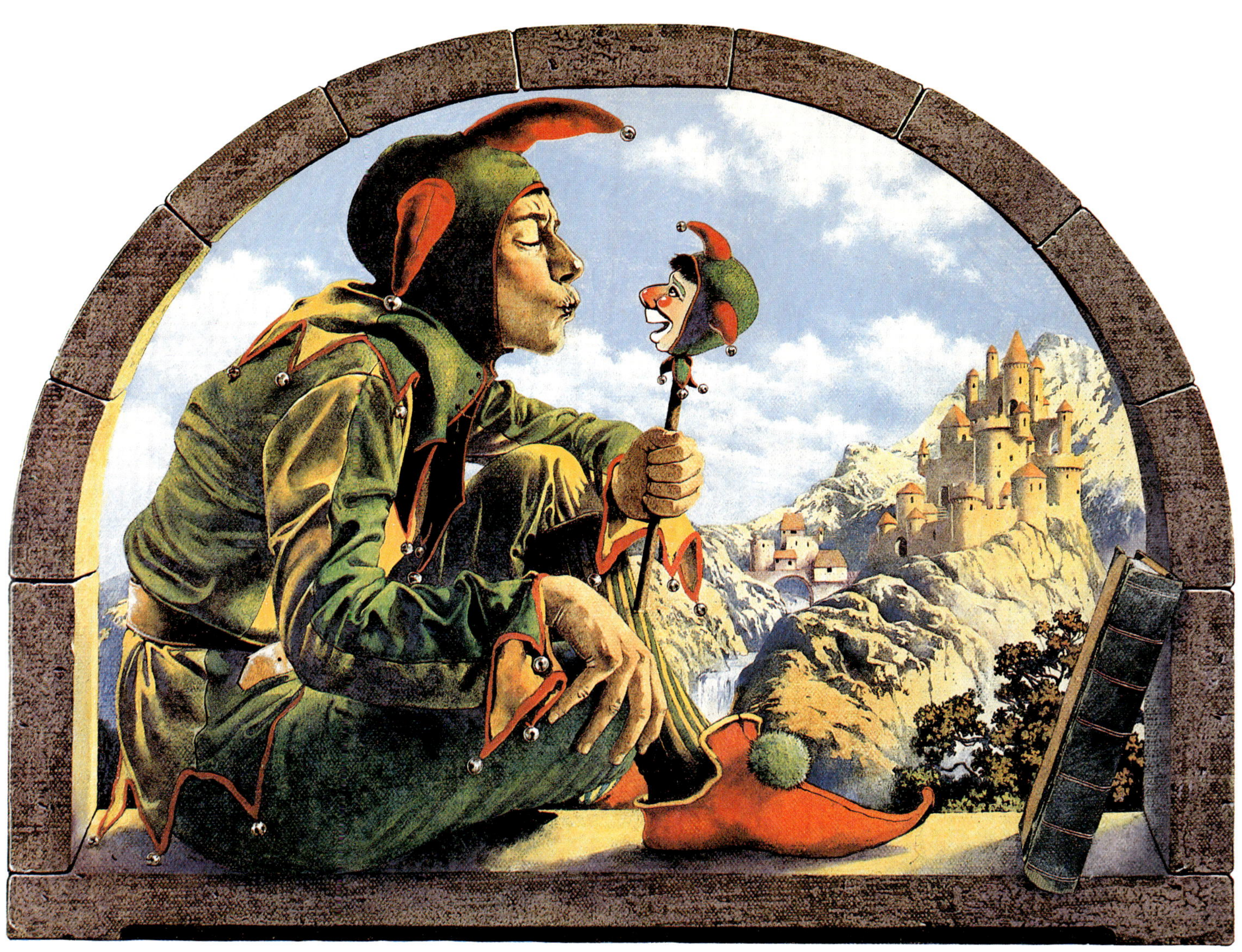

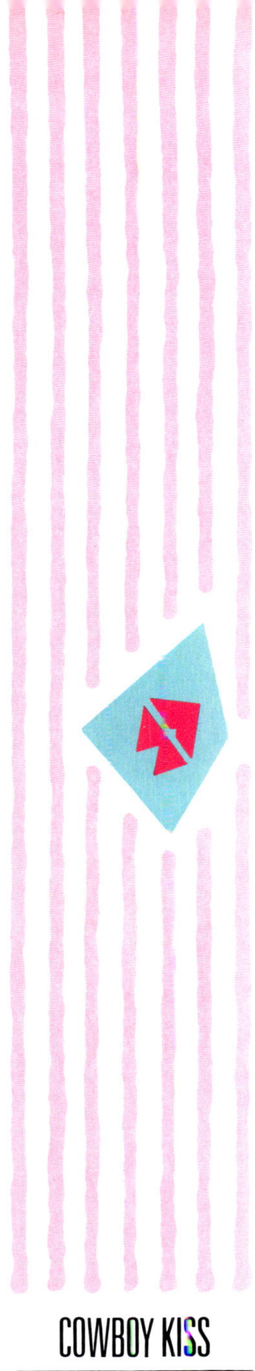

COWBOY KISS

WARREN MADILL

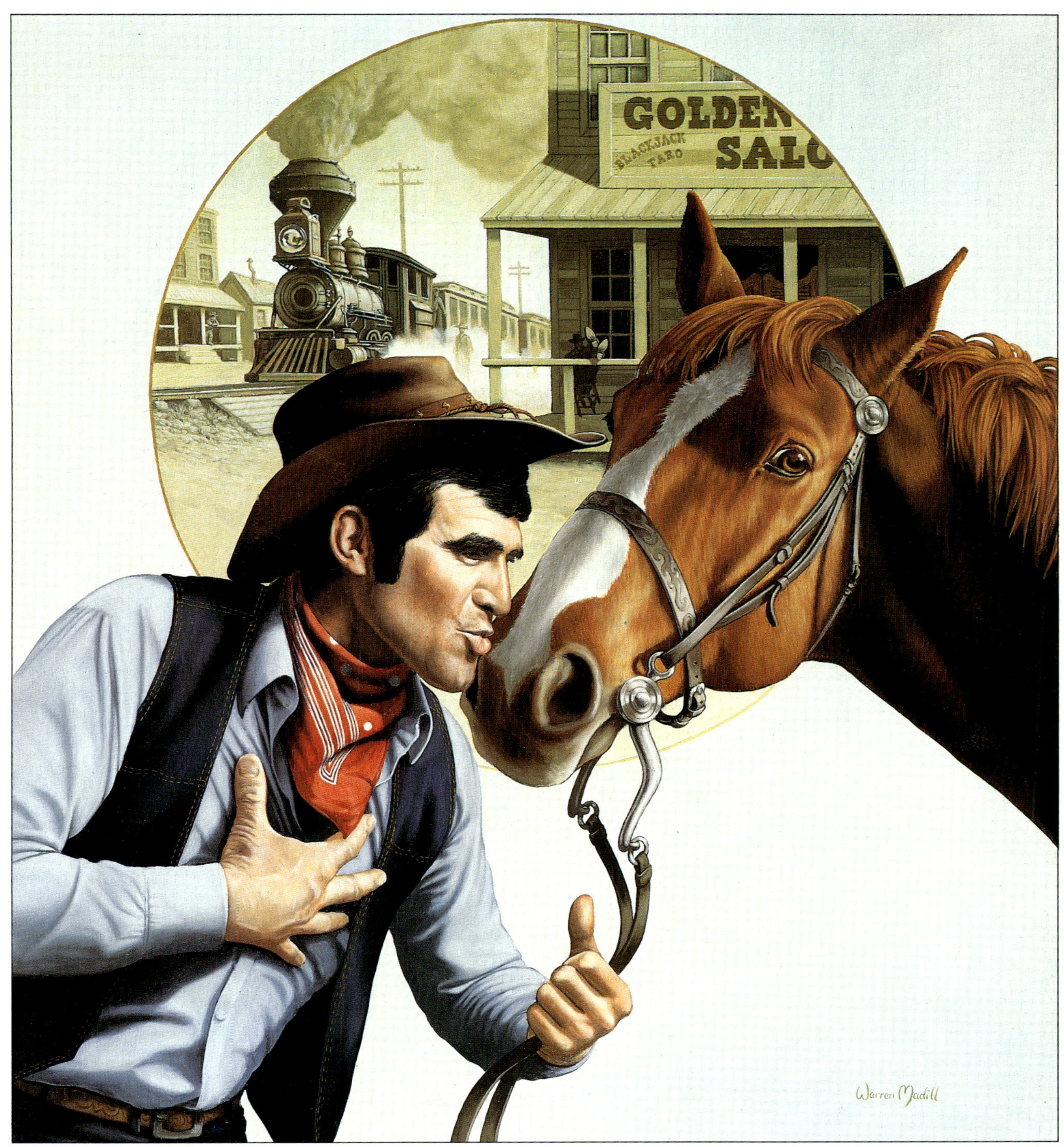
GOLDEN
SALO
BLACKJACK
FARO
Warren Madill

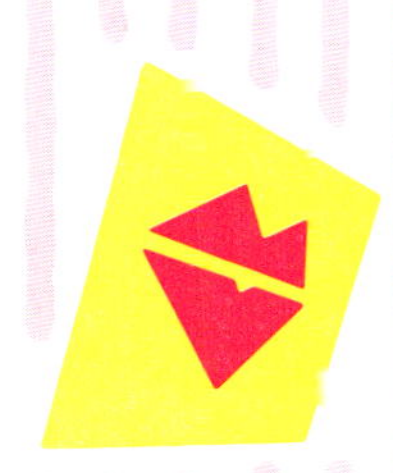

PRIMEVAL KISS

JOHN MAC

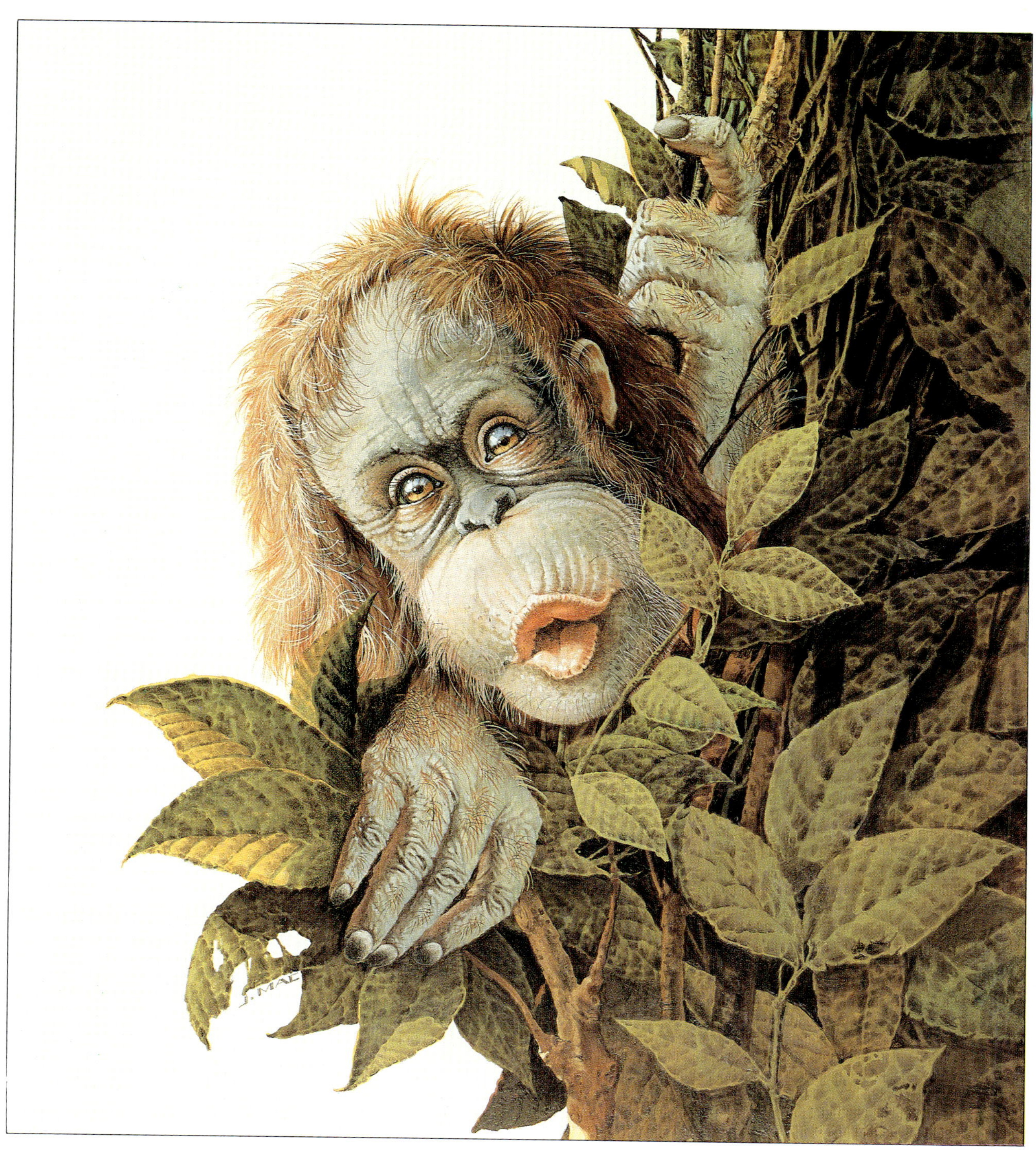

CRINGING KISS
WARREN MADILL

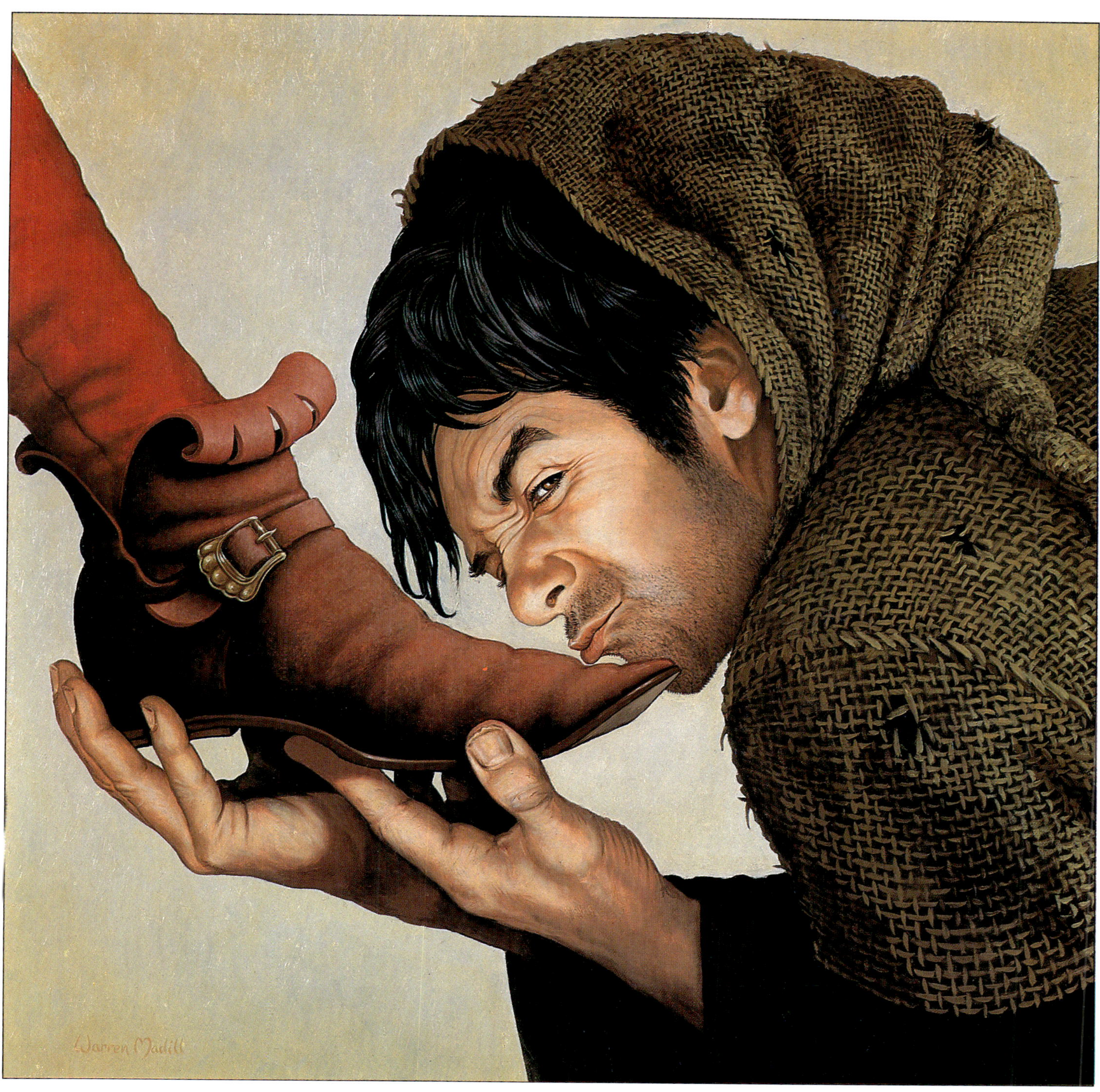
Warren Madill

LONG DISTANCE KISS

SYD BRAK

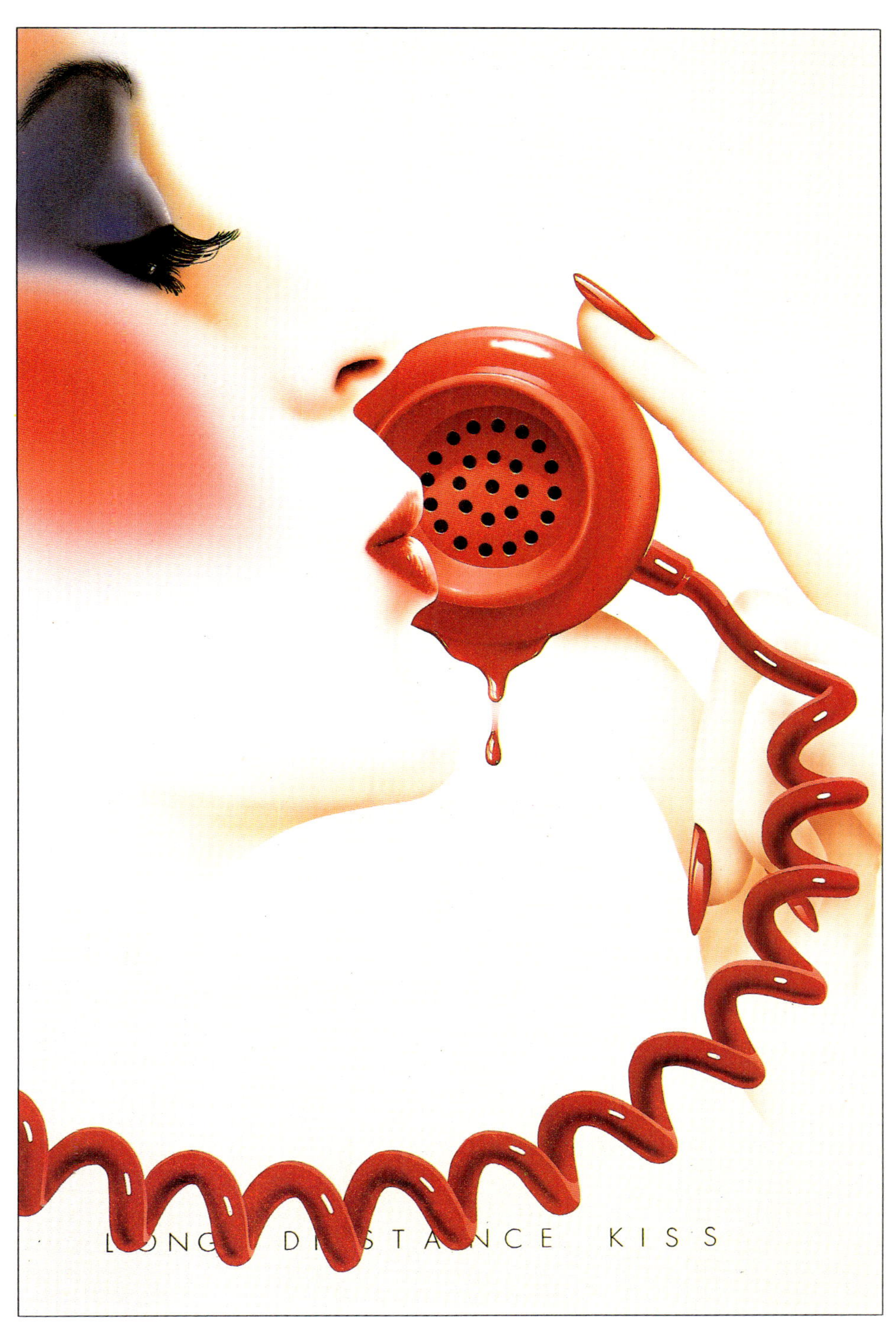
LONG DISTANCE KISS

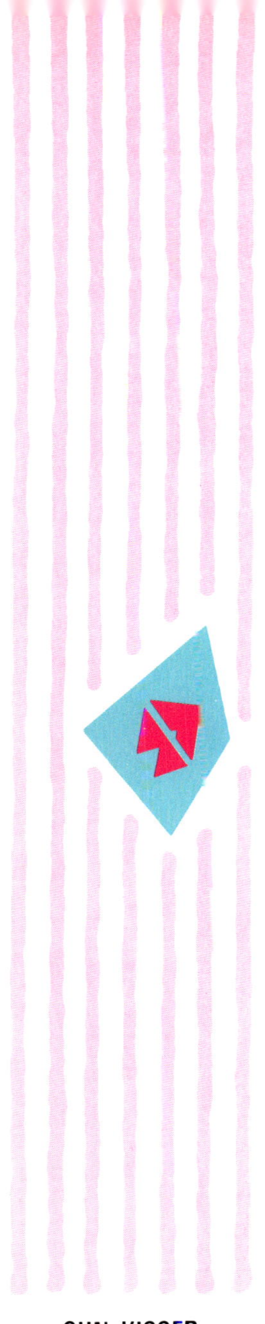

SUN-KISSED

DAVID HOLMES

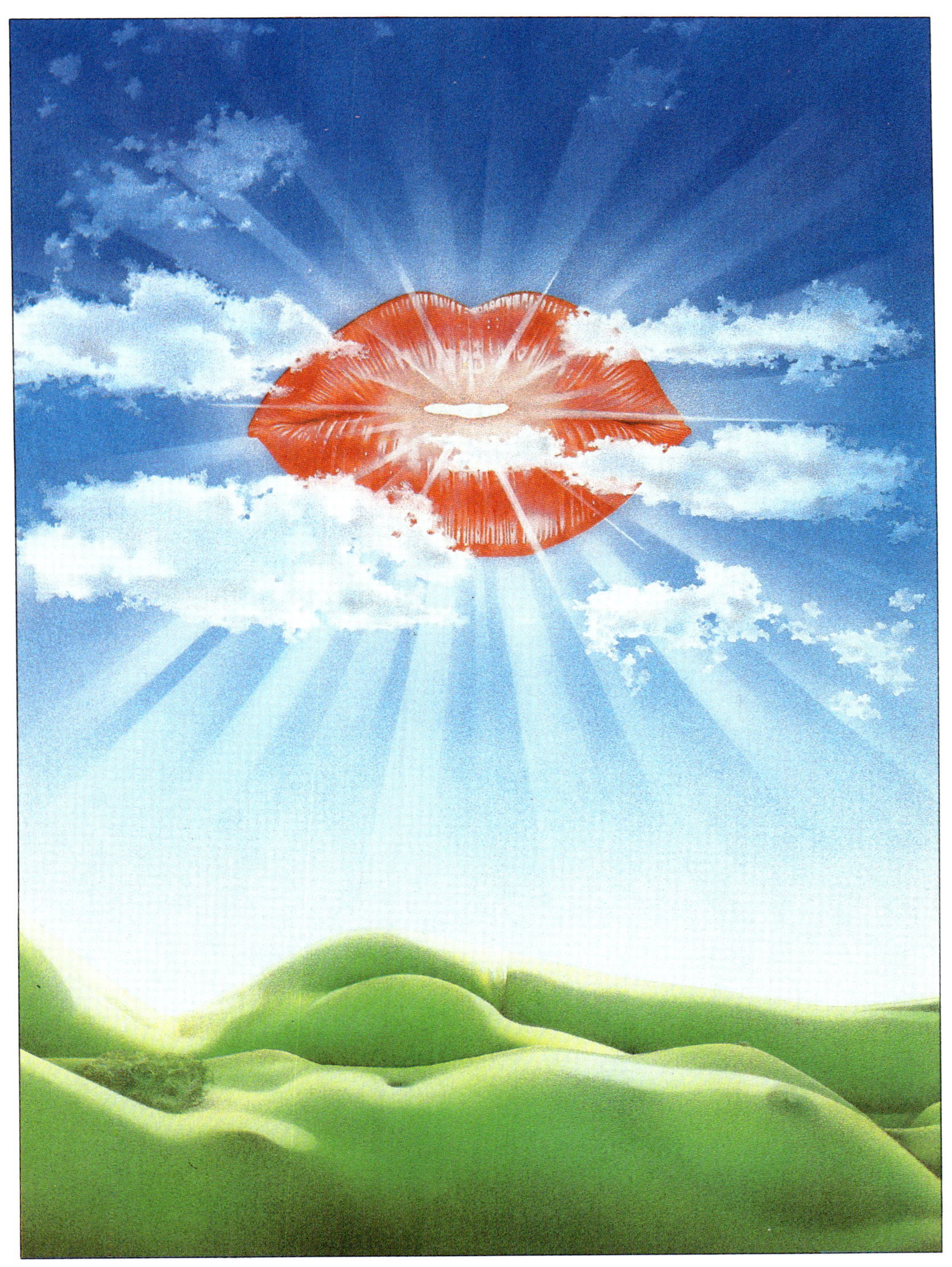

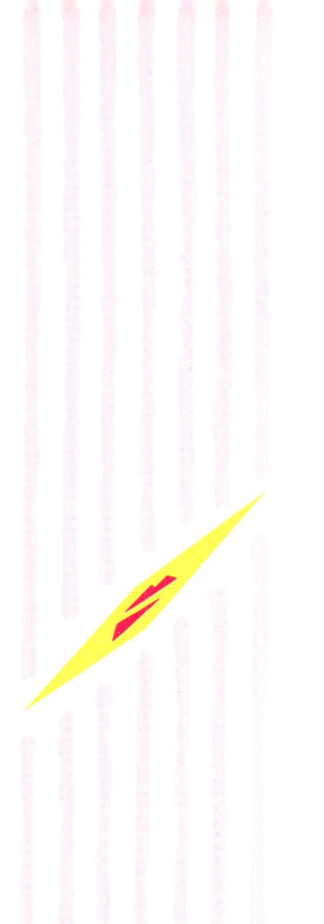

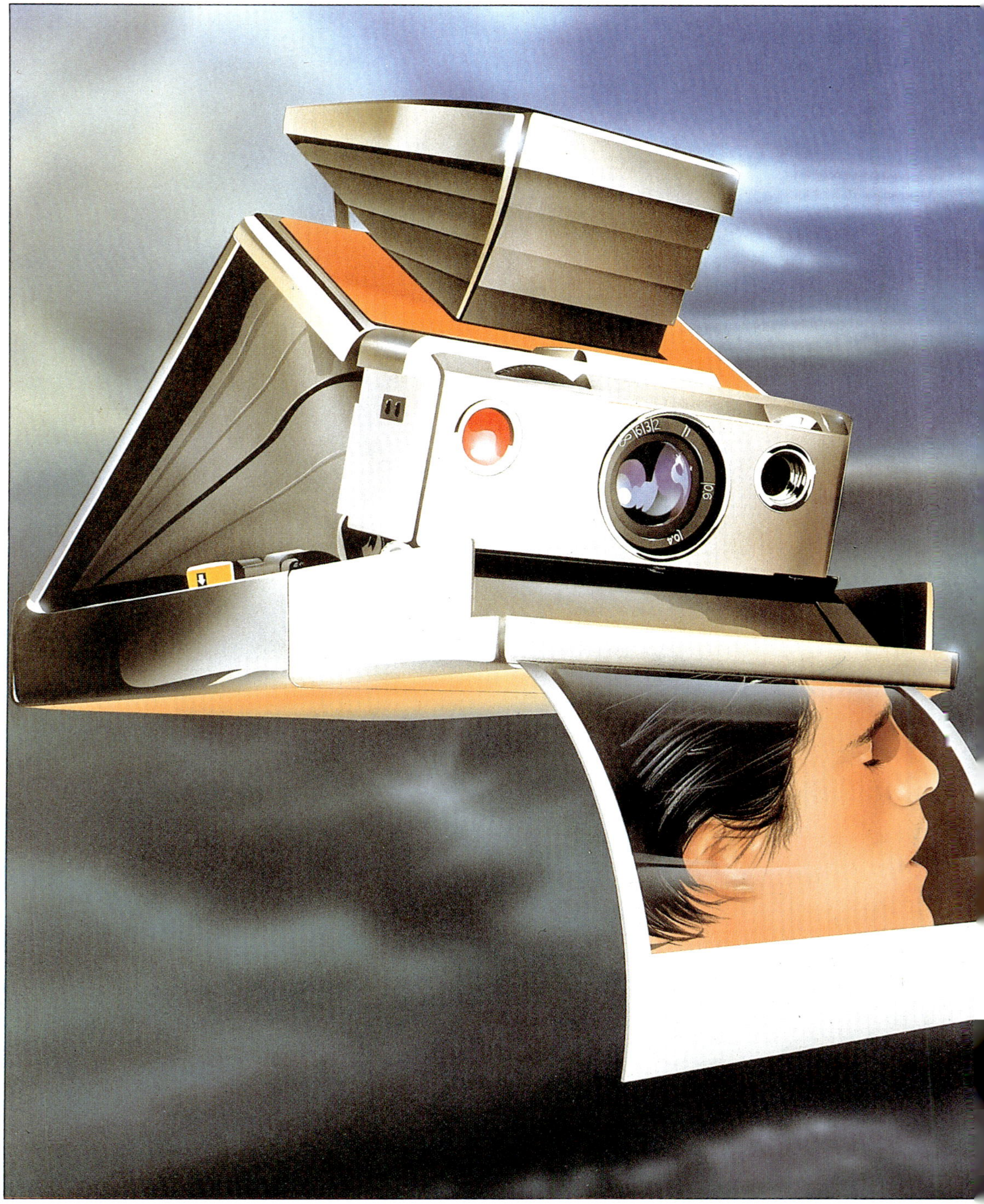

INSTANT KISS

PETE KELLY

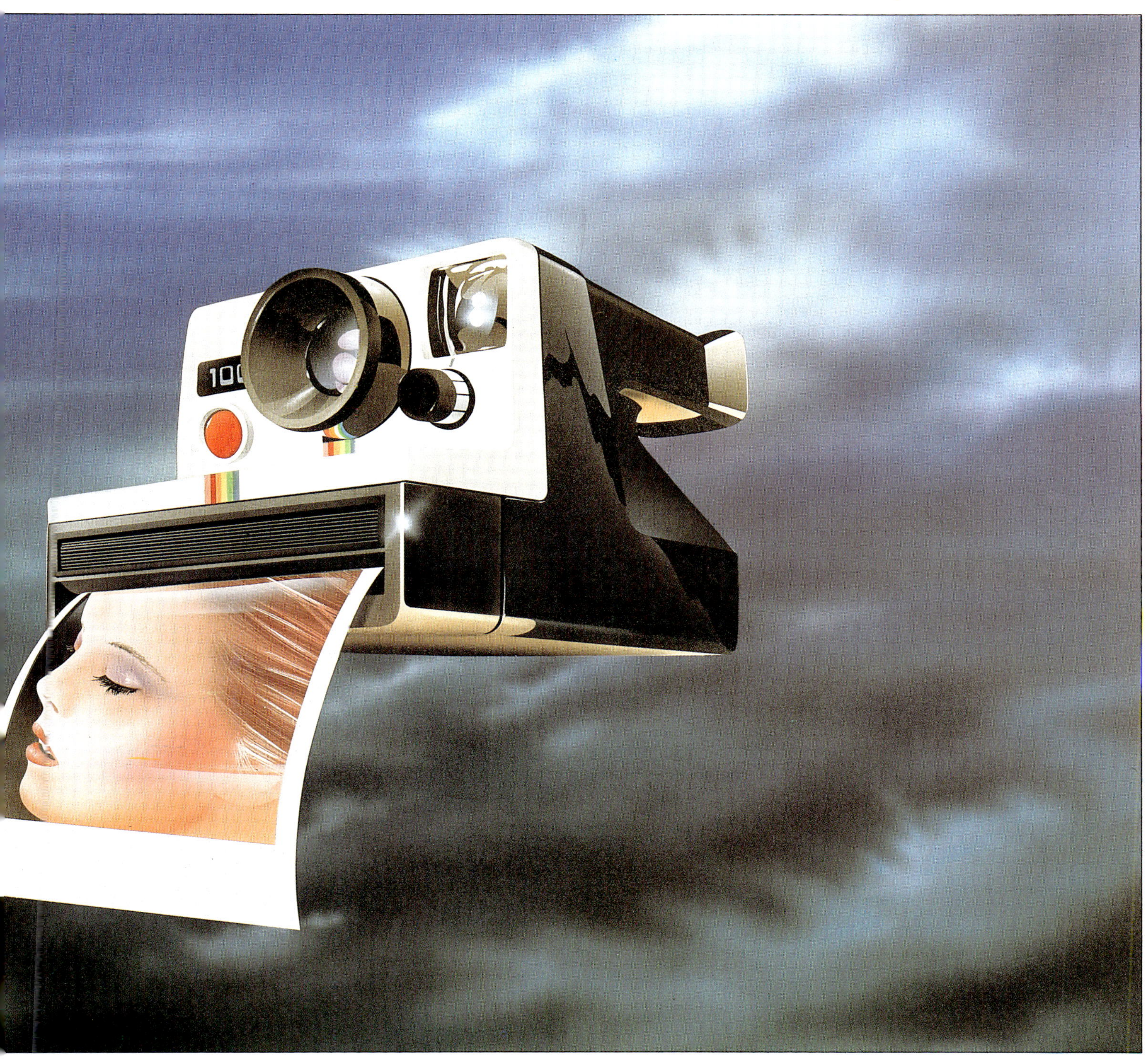

WET KISS

JEFF CUMMINS

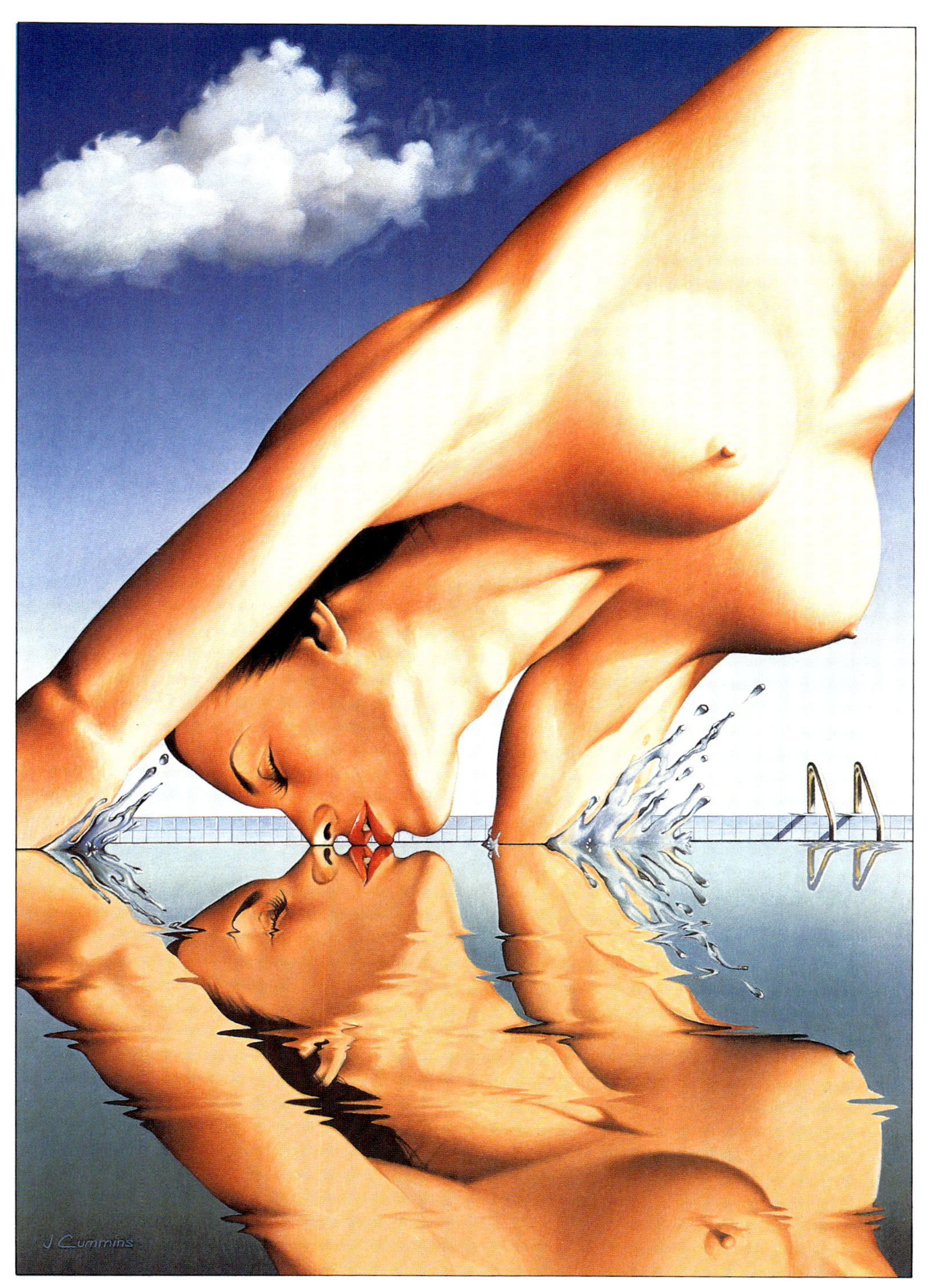
J Cummins

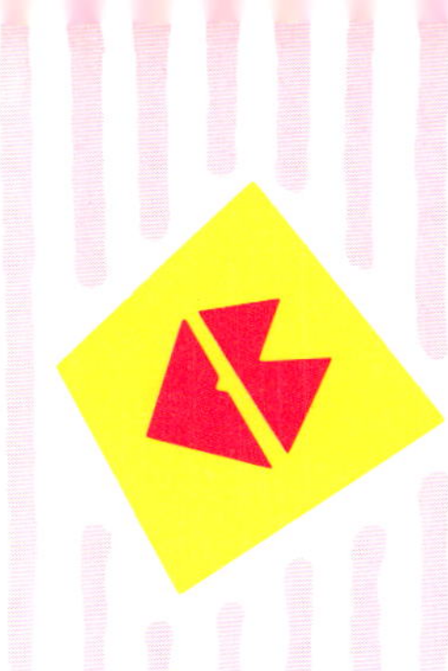

MERMAID KISS

ANDREW FARLEY

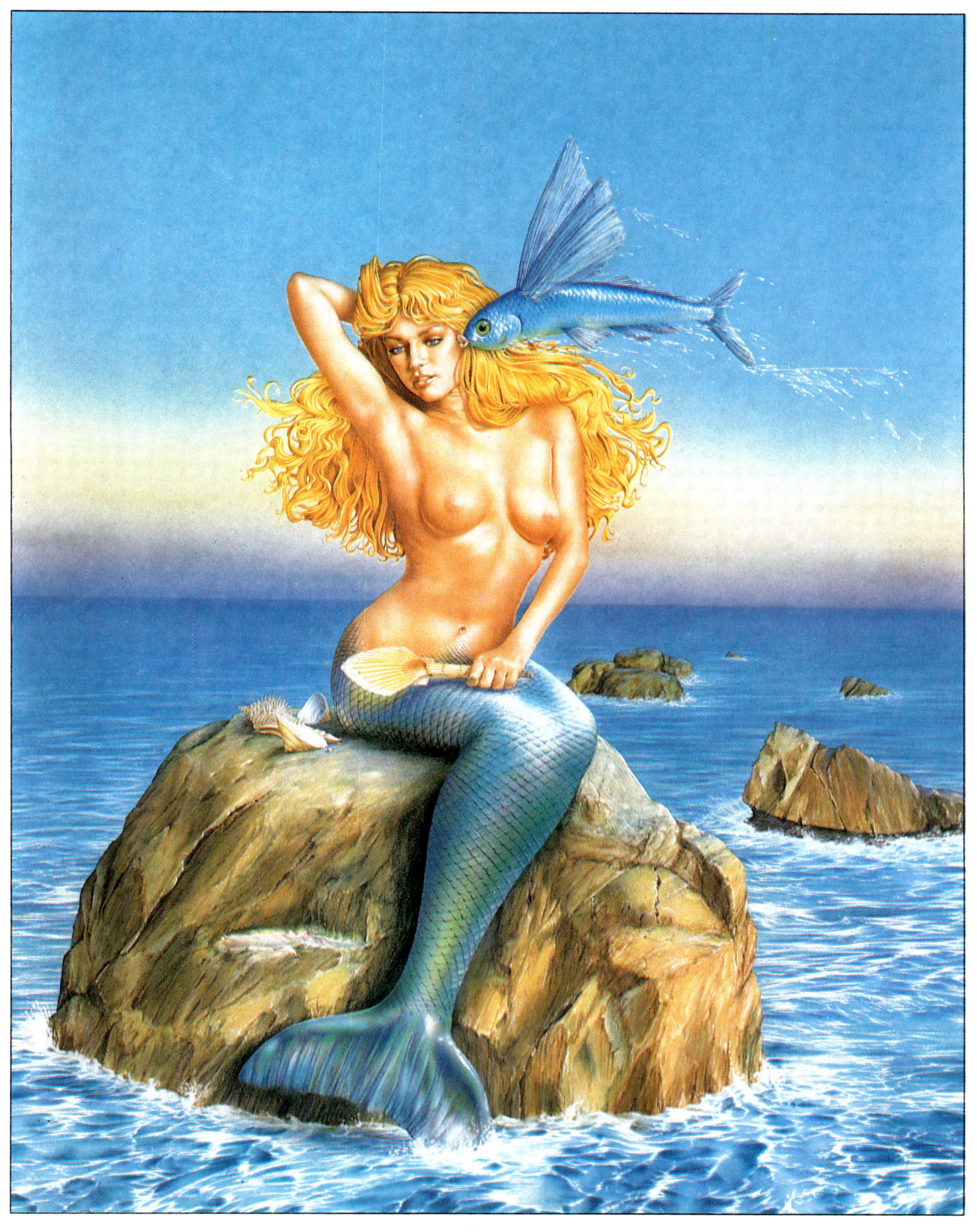

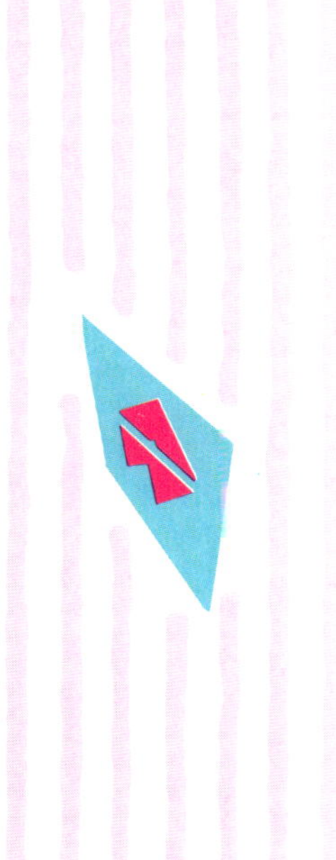

PRINCELY KISS

IRVINE PEACOCK

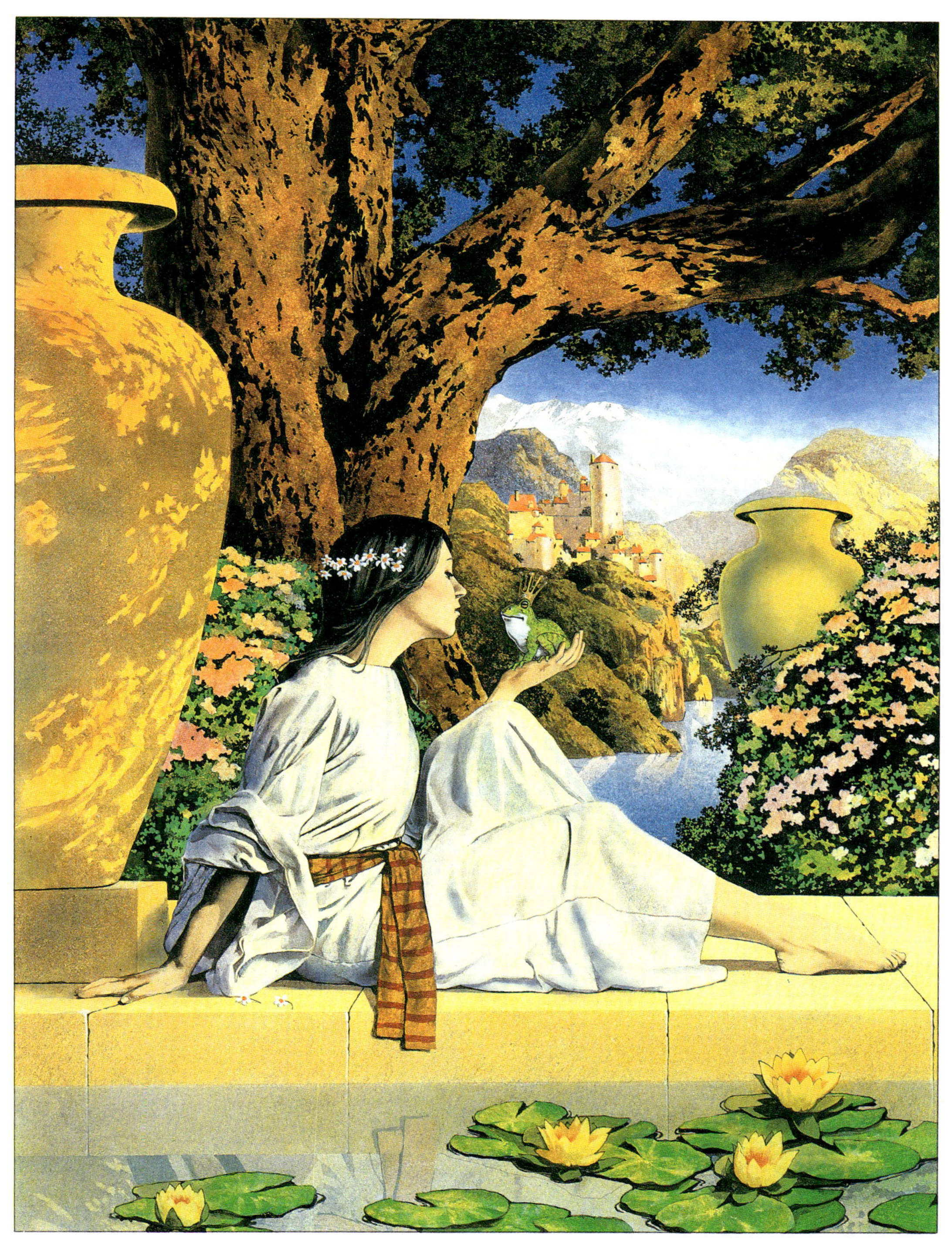

KISS OF DEATH

SYD BRAK

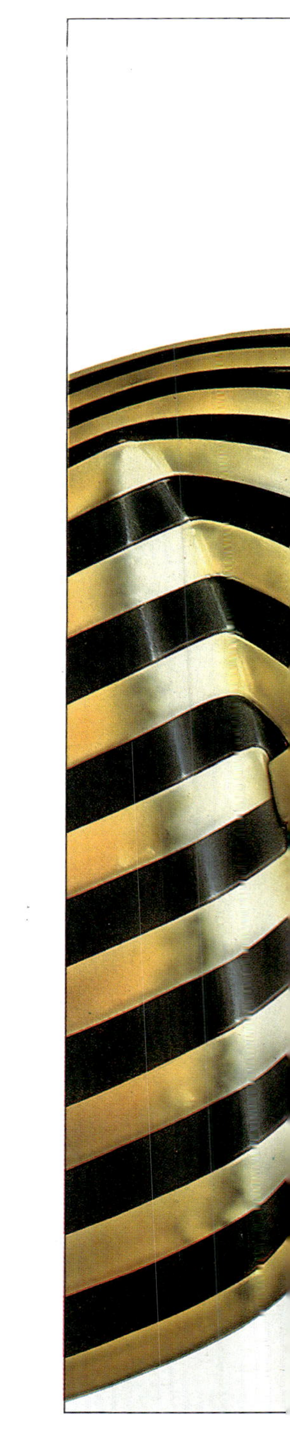

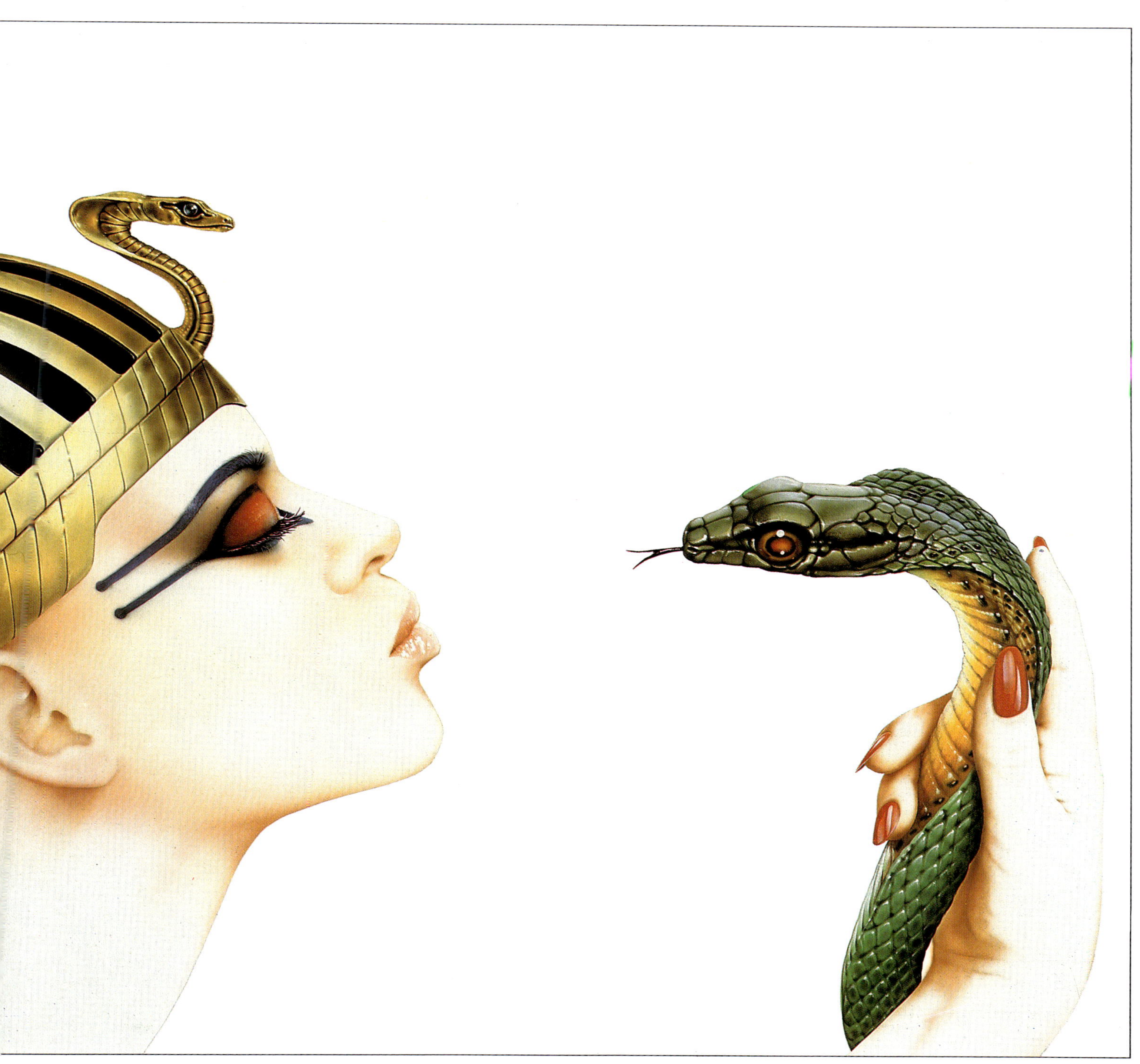

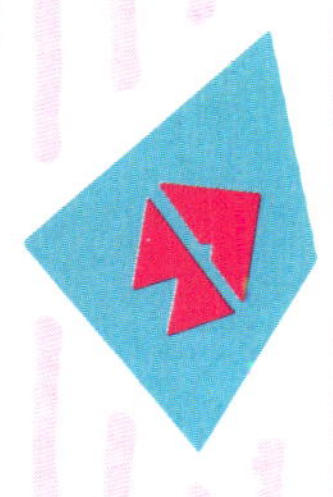

COSMIC KISS

PETE KELLY

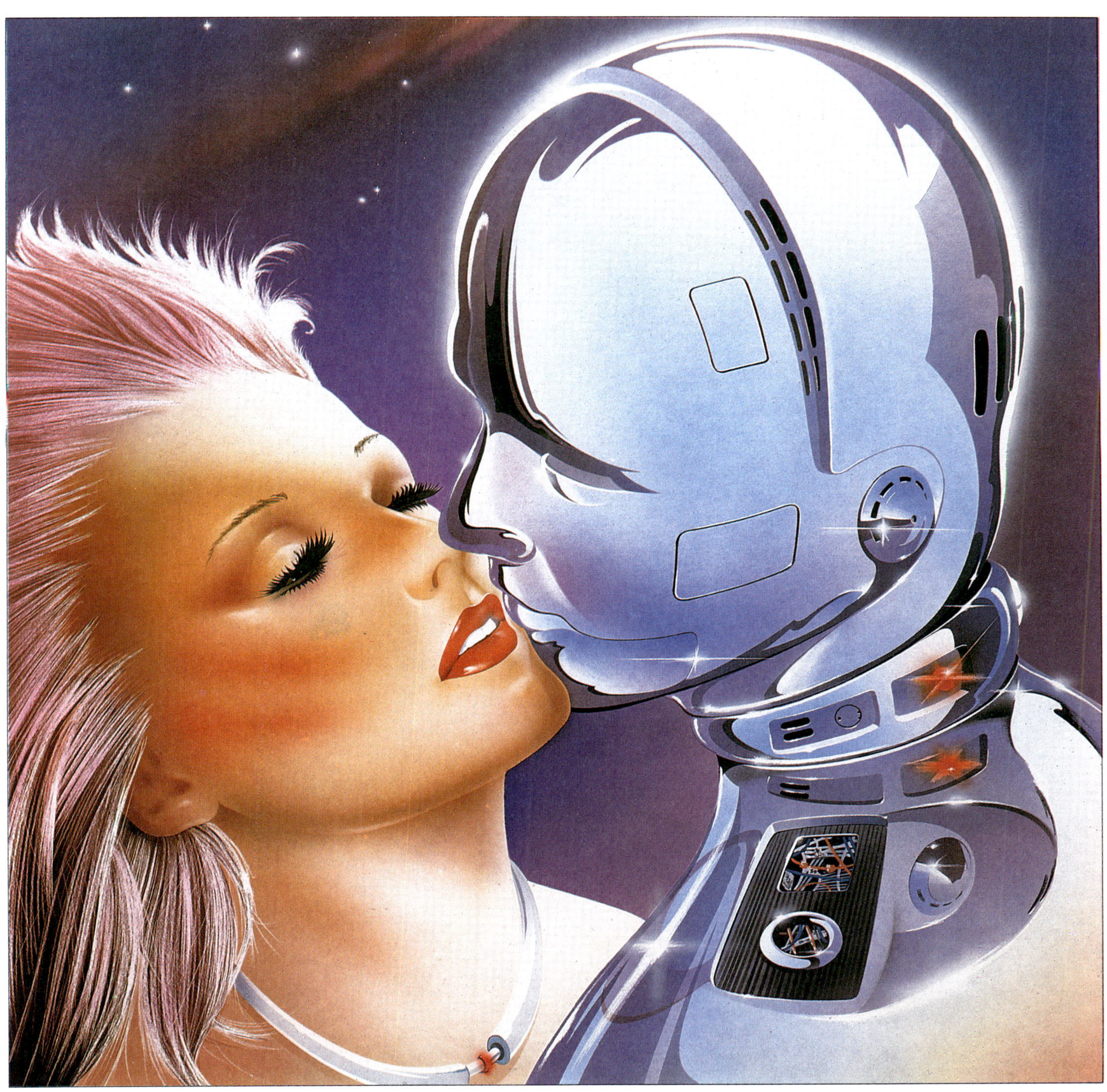

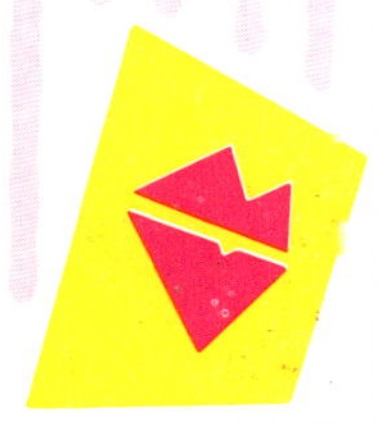

CLASSIC KISS

BARRY LEPARD

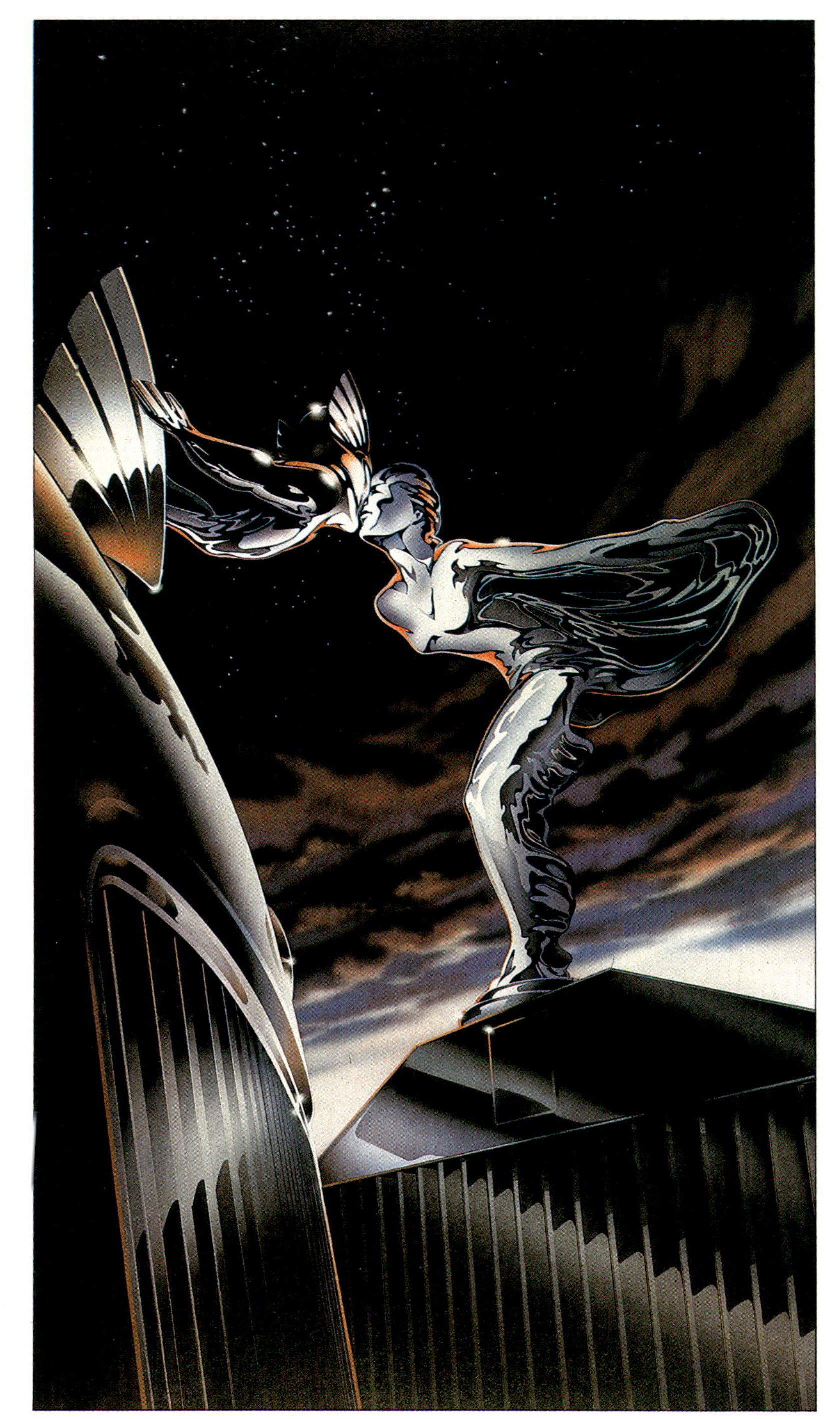

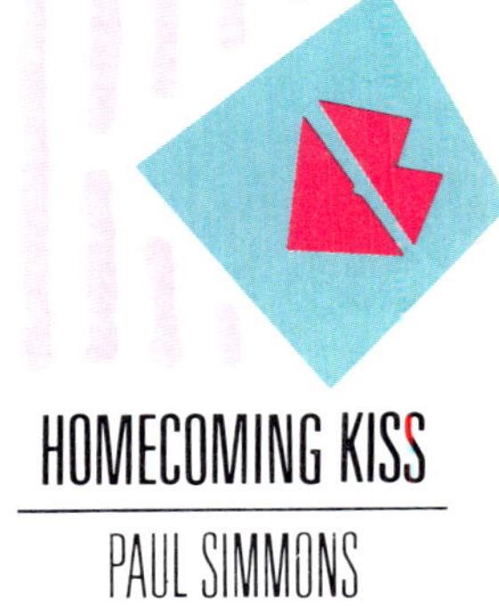

HOMECOMING KISS

PAUL SIMMONS

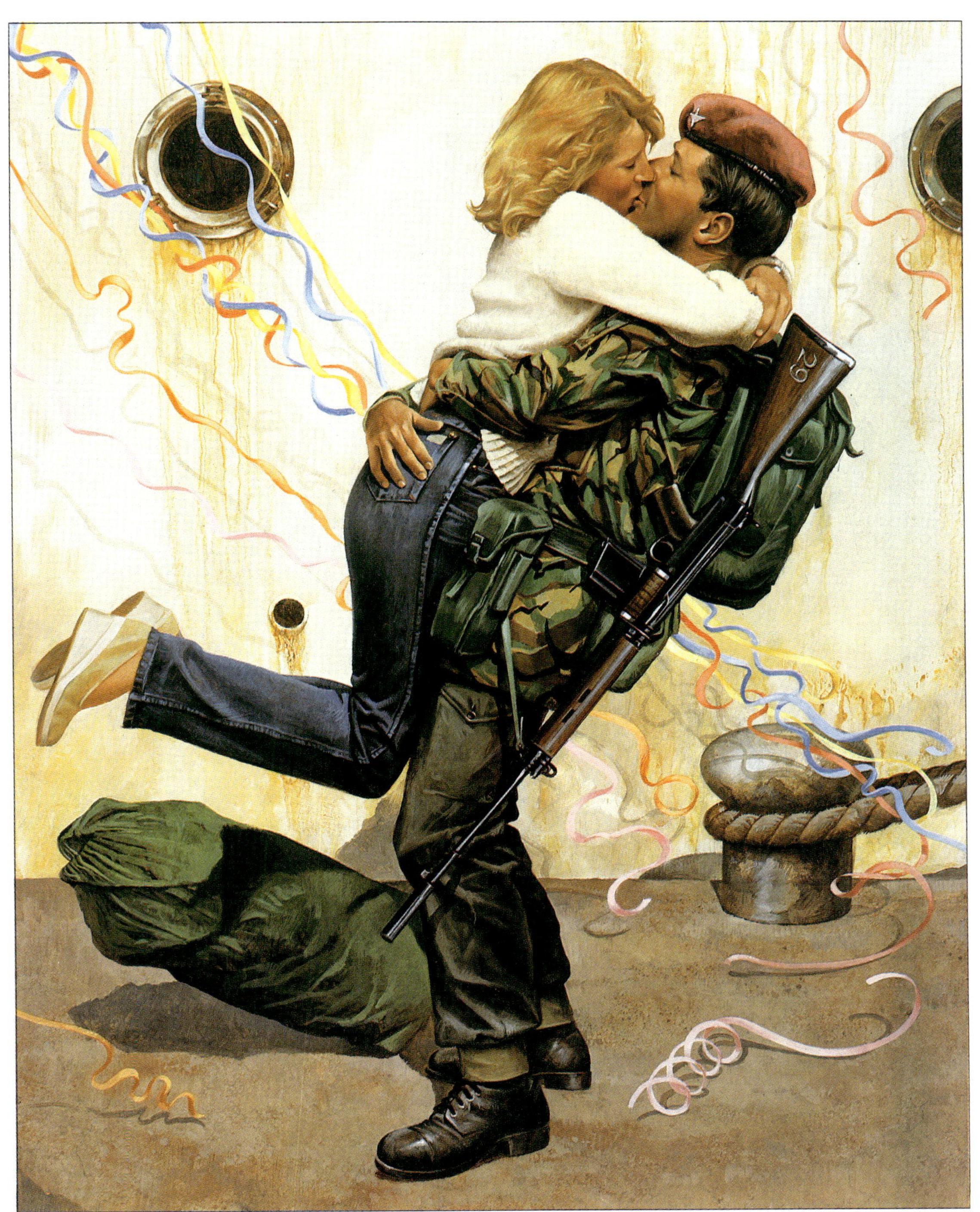
29

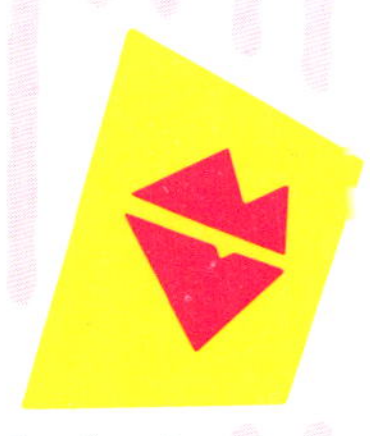

FRENCH KISS

ROGER PEARCE

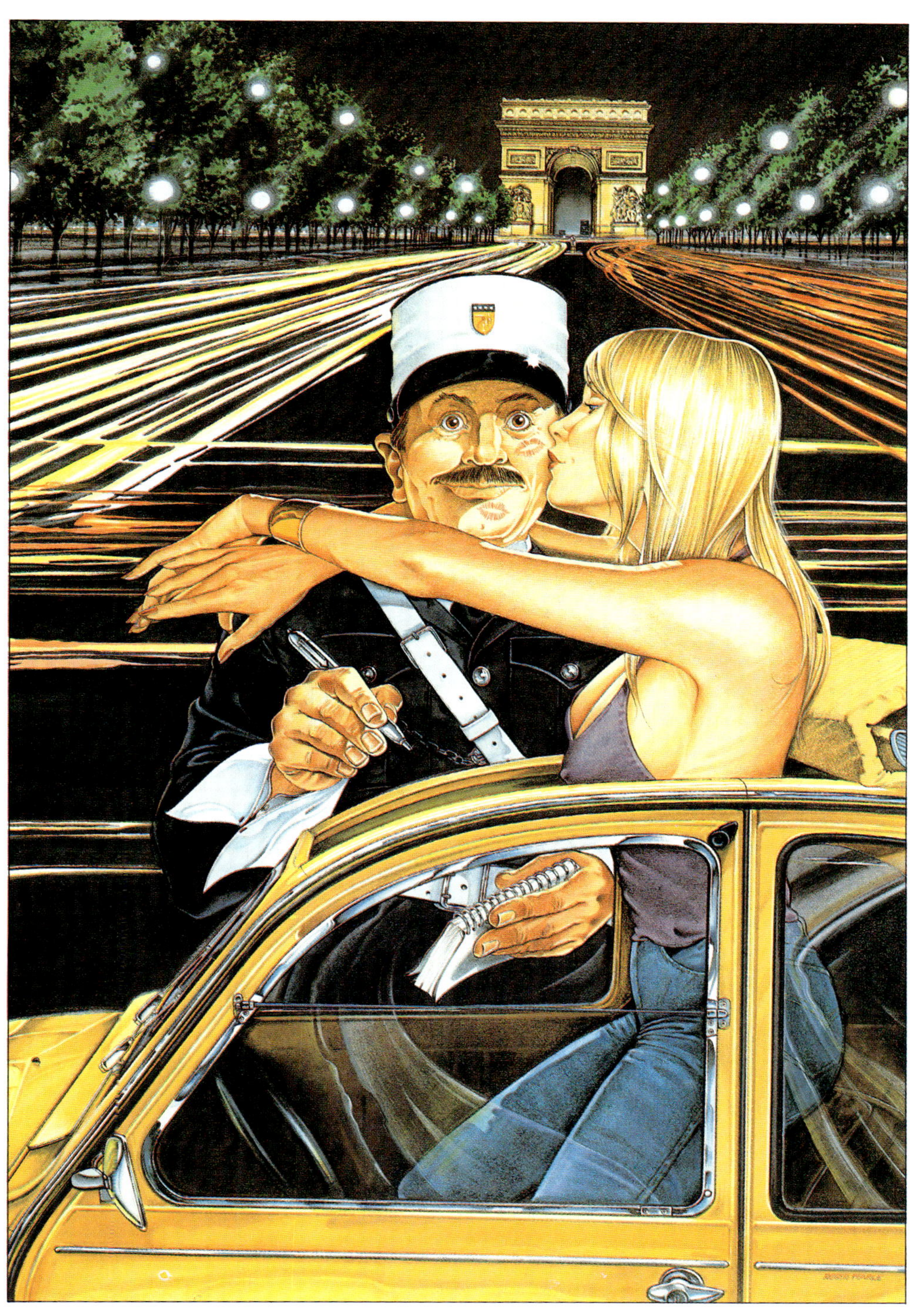

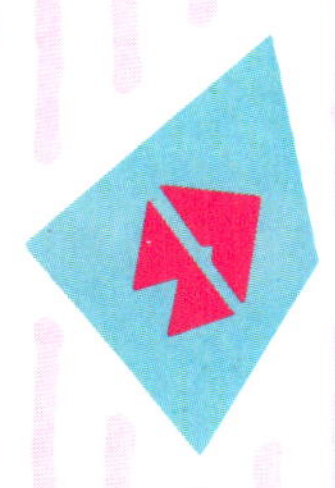

FAREWELL KISS

PAUL SIMMONS

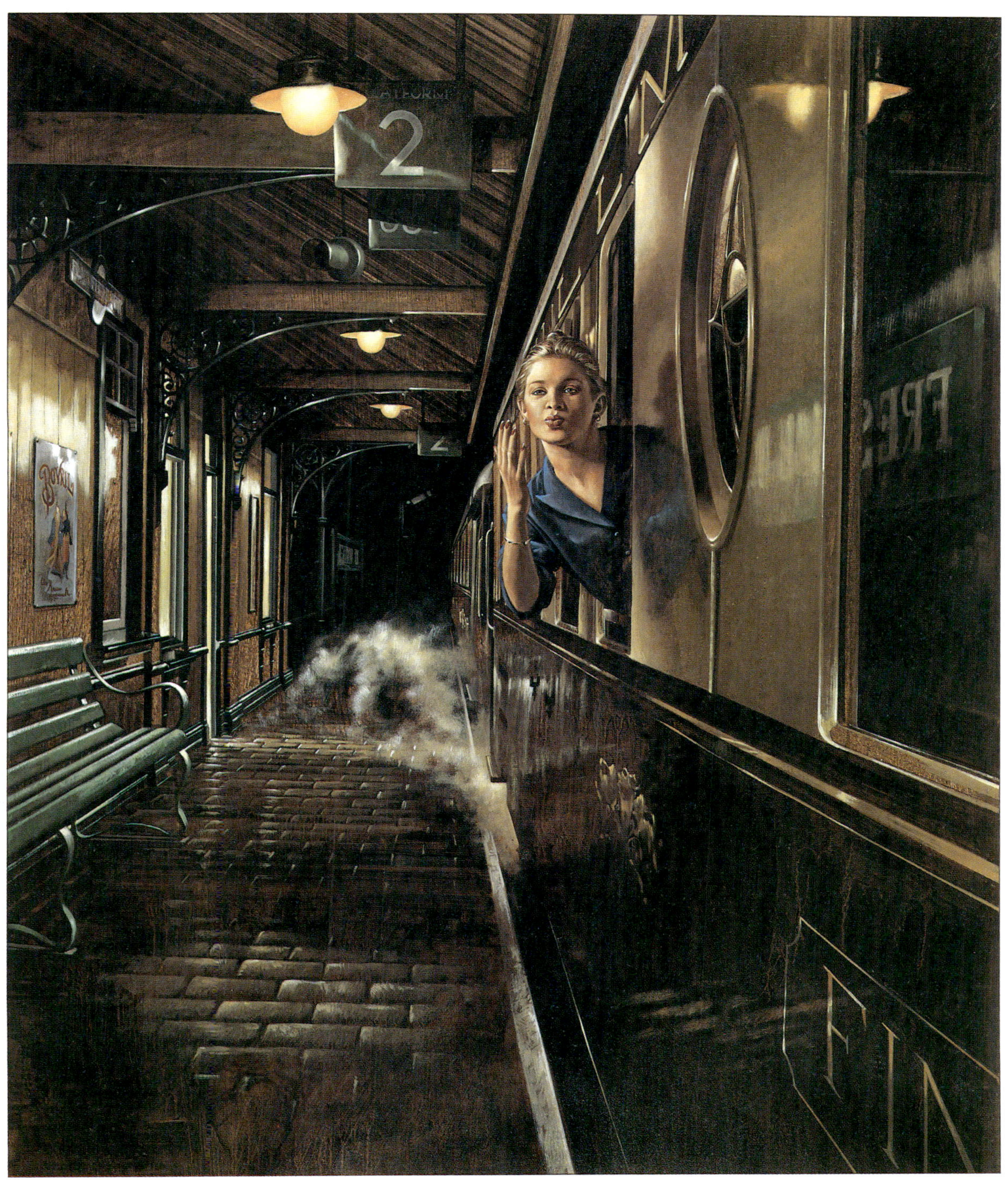
2
FIN